God's Eternal Purpose

An introduction to Christian doctrine

Peter Williams

God's Eternal Purpose: An introduction to Christian doctrine
Copyright © 2013 Peter Williams

Published by:
Swansea Valley Bible Church, Ystradgynlais, Powys, Wales, UK

All rights reserved.

No part of this publication may be reproduced, stored in a retrieval system, or transmitted in any form or by any means, electronic, mechanical, photocopying, recording, or otherwise, without prior written permission of the publisher.

Scripture taken from the THE HOLY BIBLE, NEW INTERNATIONAL VERSION®, NIV® Copyright © 1973, 1978, 1984, 2011 by Biblica, Inc.® Used by permission. All rights reserved worldwide.

ISBN: 978-1-291-54476-3

Contents

Introduction to the Study — 1
Purpose of study - Bible tools - Methods of study - True dimension of Scripture

Study 1: The Doctrine of Scripture — 3
Introduction to the course - Revelation and the Bible - General revelation - Special revelation - The inspiration & authority of Scripture - Interpretation of the Scriptures

Study 2: The Doctrine of God — 15
The existence of God - The Names of God - The attributes of God - God in Unity and Trinity

Study 3: The Doctrine of Christ — 27
Old Testament predictions - The human nature of Christ - The Divine nature of Christ - Christ as Prophet, Priest and King

Study 4: The Doctrine of Man — 37
The origin and nature of man, Body, Soul, Spirit - Man in innocence - Man in sin - Man in grace - Man in death - Man in final judgement - Man in future glory

Study 5: The Doctrine of Salvation — 45
Salvation - Atonement - Redemption - Reconciliation - Adoption - Justification - Sanctification

Study 6: The Doctrine of the Spirit — 55
Use of the word 'spirit' - The personality of the Spirit - The work of the Spirit - The Holy Spirit in the Old Testament - The Holy Spirit in the New Testament

Study 7: The Doctrine of the Kingdom of God — 65
Three aspects of the Kingdom - Adams place lost to Satan - The coming of Christ the new King - The Kingdom in the present - The Kingdom in the future

Study 8: The Doctrine of the Church — 77
What is the church? - The church as a body - The church as a bride - The church as a building - Worship in the church - Government of the church - The church in the world

Study 9: The Doctrine of Angels & Demons — 87
The origin and nature of angels - The different orders of angels - The holy angels - The Devil and his angels

Study 10: The Doctrine of the Last Things — 97
Different views among Christians - The promise of Christ's return - The incentives of his coming - Signs of his coming - The Millennial reign - The final judgement

Appendix 1: Problem Texts in the Bible — 107

Appendix 2: Bible Reference Abbreviations — 109

Bibliography — 110

Acknowledgement

I want to record my appreciation to Mrs. Pat Davies for her patient and helpful proof reading of this book, and the work of checking and re-checking carried out by my wife Jenny.

God's Eternal Purpose

Introduction to the Study

Purpose of Bible study

The following studies are meant to be an introduction to some of the major doctrines in the Scripture. They are designed to give some structure to help people with an interest in searching out the truth of God's word. As we look at each great truth a theme develops which holds all the doctrines together. It is the theme of 'God's Eternal Purpose' which runs right through Scripture.

Your study of the Bible will be as big as you want to make it. You never come to a place where you know it all. No man-made system of theology ever perfectly presents the fullness of truth in Scripture. Remember that this course is only an introduction to the teachings of Scripture. I trust it will inspire you to seek to know the Bible better, and beyond that, to know the God of the Bible better. All study must serve a purpose. It is not just gathering Bible information. That knowledge has to make an impact on our lives and lead us to maturity in our Christian walk.

   a) The study of Scripture should lead us to more intimacy with God through His Son - it should lead us to worship.

   b) It should develop a longing to become more like Christ and develop us in character - it should lead to maturity.

   c) Knowledge of the Scripture should help us communicate the gospel more clearly - it should lead to others coming to know God's Son, Jesus Christ.

   d) It should enlarge our understanding of life and give meaning to our existence - it should lead to a fulfilment of the purpose for which we were born.

Helpful tools in Bible study

There are many useful tools that have been produced in order to help us discover the great truths of the Bible. There are Concordances, which gives us a reference for every word in the Bible and the meaning of those words. A Bible Dictionary will introduce us to the many topics, places and people in the Bible. A Commentary (whole Bible) will bring out the general teaching that each book has to give and show its setting in the Scriptures. Commentaries vary greatly in length, with some being written on just one chapter of the Bible. A Book on Systematic Theology will develop our understanding of the great doctrines of Scripture and set them out in order for study.

Methods used in studying the Bible

Thematic – Grace, Covenant, Kingdom etc.

Characters – Joseph, David, Christ etc.

Book Study – Deuteronomy, Isaiah, Galatians etc.

Chronological History – Time line of events in the Bible.

Systematic Theology – Setting out doctrines in an orderly way.

Your involvement in the Studies

Throughout the studies there are several questions given which are meant to help the student look at some of the issues raised. Time spent in doing this will help impress the truth on the mind. Students will get far more benefit from the studies if they spend some time and effort in doing this.

The true dimension of Scripture

The truth of the Bible is multi-dimensional:

1. We can take a scripture statement, it constitutes a truth. It is like a straight line which gives us one dimension of the truth.

2. If we gather several statements of Scripture and link them together they begin to make a doctrine. It is like four straight lines making a rectangle and shows truth in two dimensions.

3. We then work out the implications of doctrine and apply it to life to make it relevant and practical. This brings truth into a third dimension. In our illustration we now have a solid object.

4. There is an added dimension when the Holy Spirit sheds light on truth and gives us revelation of its wonder and value. This fills the word with light, life and power. As Jesus said, "The Spirit gives life; the flesh counts for nothing. The words I have spoken to you--they are full of the Spirit and life." (Jhn 6:63). The writer of Hebrews adds, "For the word of God is alive and active. Sharper than any double-edged sword, it penetrates even to dividing soul and spirit, joints and marrow; it judges the thoughts and attitudes of the heart." (Heb 4:12).

The Bible is a revelation from God, about God and his redemptive purpose in Christ. Until it becomes a revelation to us we will not understand its true meaning.

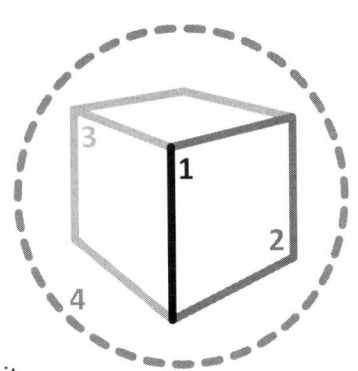

God's Eternal Purpose

Study 1
The Doctrine of Scripture

📖 **Psalm 119:89-104**

We are setting out to answer two questions

1. Why do we need the Bible?
2. What do we believe about the Bible?

Revelation and the Scriptures

How can we know the truth about God and his purpose in the world? We are faced with the fact that "in the wisdom of God, the world through wisdom did not know God" (1 Cor 1:21). There are two main reasons why we cannot discover God by our own initiative.

1. God is too great for us to understand by human logic. How can we grasp the greatness of the infinity and eternity of God? His absolute holiness sets him so far above us that we cannot comprehend him.
2. Our fallenness has so affected human nature that all our faculties of mind, emotion and intuition are flawed. To discover God for ourselves is an utter impossibility.

The only way that God can be known is if he graciously chooses to reveal himself. God can stoop down to us, but we cannot reach up to him. Has God chosen to reveal himself? The answer is yes, and the Bible tells us about that revelation.

God can stoop down to us, but we cannot reach up to God

Dr. M Lloyd-Jones describes revelation as *"the act by which God communicates to human beings the truth concerning himself, his nature, works and purpose."*

The way that God has revealed himself to mankind is usually divided into two parts, 1) General Revelation 2) Special Revelation.

General revelation

God has revealed himself through his works of creation and in the way he sustains all of creation in his providence. Paul used the theme of creation when speaking to the people of Lystra. He said, "We are bringing you good news, telling you to turn from these worthless things to the living God, who made the heavens and the earth and the sea and everything in them." (Act 14:15). The Psalmist said long ago, "The heavens declare the glory of God; the skies proclaim the work of his hands." (Psa 19:1). All people are left without excuse before God if they do not acknowledge him, "For since the creation of the world God's invisible qualities--his eternal power and divine nature--have been clearly seen, being understood from what has been made, so that people are without excuse." (Rom 1:19-20).

People are left without an excuse because God not only reveals himself objectively in creation, outside of mankind, he also reveals himself subjectively in conscience, within mankind. Paul deals with this issue and says, "(..They show that the requirements of the law are written on their hearts, their consciences also bearing witness, and their thoughts sometimes accusing them and at other times even defending them.)" (Rom 2:15). Through these two witnesses God is revealing to all mankind, firstly, that he exists, and secondly, that all people are answerable to him.

Because our fallen state has affected our minds and hearts the revelation that God has made of himself in creation and conscience are not sufficient to meet our need. Mankind everywhere distorts this revelation of God and ends up subduing conscience and worshipping the creature rather than the creator. "For although they knew God, they neither glorified him as God nor gave thanks to him ... and exchanged the glory of the immortal God for images made to look like a mortal human being and birds and animals and reptiles." (Rom 1:21-23).

Assignment

How should we use the theme of God's revelation in creation and conscience to preach the gospel? (see Act 14:8-18 & Act 17:16-31)

Special revelation

Our great need is for a revelation of God beyond what he has shown us in creation. The knowledge of God in creation, in itself, is not sufficient to save us.

That special revelation is given to us in the Bible. The Bible stands unique among all the literature of the world. It reveals to us the character and nature of God, and his great eternal plan to restore a people to his favour, through redemption. This unique book is divine in its nature because it is God's inspired message for all people in every generation. Yet, the Bible remains a human book, in the sense that God chose to speak through ordinary men within their own culture and time in history. He used their personalities to communicate the message he wanted them to bring.

> *The Bible stands unique among all the literature of the world.*

The Bible opens out for us the various ways in which God has revealed himself over the centuries, "In the past God spoke to our ancestors through the prophets at **many times** and in **various ways**, but in these last days he has spoken to us by his Son" (Heb 1:1-2).

God has revealed himself:-

   a) Through theophanies (or Christophanies), in which God manifested himself, in visible form, as the angel of the LORD. He came to Abraham (Gen 18:1-15), to Gideon

(Jdg 6:11-14), Samson's parents (Jdg 13:1-5) etc.

b) Through God speaking directly to people in an audible voice. He spoke to Adam and Eve, "Then the man and his wife heard the sound of the LORD God as he was walking in the garden in the cool of the day ... But the LORD God called to the man, 'Where are you'?" (Gen 3:8-9). He spoke to Noah, "So God said to Noah, "I am going to put an end to all people, for the earth is filled with violence because of them." (Gen 6:13-14). He spoke to Moses on Mt. Sinai, "and the LORD said to him, 'Go down and warn the people so they do not force their way through to see the LORD'" (Exo 19:20-21).

c) Through miraculous signs and wonders as the God who could intervene in the issues of life. He came in such a way to bring about the birth of Isaac, "Sarah became pregnant and bore a son to Abraham in his old age, at the very time God had promised him." (Gen 21:1-7). He came to Moses and spoke through the ten plagues on Egypt, (Exo 7-11). He revealed himself through Elijah with fire from heaven, "Then the fire of the LORD fell and burned up the sacrifice, the wood, the stones and the soil, and also licked up the water in the trench" (1 Kgs 18:37-39). He revealed himself through Elisha and the raising of a boy from the dead, (2 Kgs 4:32-35).

d) Through visions and dreams, as Elihu says, "For God does speak--now one way, now another--though no one perceives it. In a dream, in a vision of the night, when deep sleep falls on people as they slumber in their beds" (Job 33:14-16) He spoke to Jacob at Bethel through a dream, "He had a dream in which he saw a stairway resting on the earth, with its top reaching to heaven, and the angels of God were ascending and descending on it." (Gen 28:12-17). Isaiah saw a vision of God on a throne, "In the year that King Uzziah died, I saw the Lord, high and exalted, seated on a throne; and the train of his robe filled the temple." (Isa 6:1-4); as did Ezekiel, "while I was among the exiles by the Kebar River, the heavens were opened and I saw visions of God." (Eze 1:1).

e) Through the inspired word that came to the prophets. Isaiah saw the word, "This is what Isaiah son of Amoz saw concerning Judah and Jerusalem" (Isa 2:1); while the word of the LORD came to Jeremiah, "The word of the LORD came to me" (Jer 2:1).

f) Through acts of deliverance. The whole account of God using Moses to rescue his people from Egypt, the crossing of the Red Sea and their coming to Mt. Sinai was a revelation of God as a Redeemer. This whole drama is spoken of over and over in the Old Testament. God used it to remind Israel that they were a redeemed people. This is recorded in Psalms 78, 95, 105, 106 and the prophets (Isa 11:16, Jer 7:22, 11:3-7, 34:13, Eze 20:5-8), and in many other places.

g) All these revelations of God lead up to the greatest of all, "But when the set time had fully come, God sent his Son, born of a woman, born under the law, to redeem those under the law," (Gal 4:4). The revelation of God in his Son, Jesus Christ, is the full and final revelation of all that God wants to reveal to us. In the birth, life, death and resurrection of Jesus Christ the revelation of God and his purpose is complete.

All these matters are recorded for us in the Holy Scriptures. So, we have in the Bible a truly remarkable and unique revelation of God and his redemptive plan. There is no other book like it in the entire world. The Bible is the Word of God, given in the words of men, in history.

The inspiration of the Scriptures

The verbal inspiration of the Bible has to do with the way truth was received by the writers and written down. We believe that the whole of the Bible is inspired by God. When we speak of the Bible as being 'inspired' we do not mean that it was written by men who felt inspired, such as poets. The Bible was written by men 'inspired by God' it was 'God breathed', "All Scripture is God-breathed" (2 Tim 3:16). We do not know exactly how God preserved his word from human error. However, we do know that the writers were not in a trance and taken over like robots. Nor did God dictate every word to the writers while they blindly wrote it down. God used their personalities and understanding of life to convey the truth and yet kept them from error.

So, the Bible was written fully by men, and yet was fully inspired by God.

✎ Assignment
What are some of the benefits believers receive from studying the Bible?

God used some forty different writers, over a period of more than 1500 years, to write the different books of the Bible. The amazing thing is that all these writers, separated by centuries, brought a message that never contradicted the other writers. Together they form one message that reveals the whole purpose of God for all time.

- **The Bible is called the Holy Scriptures** – "the gospel he promised beforehand through his prophets in the Holy Scriptures" (Rom 1:2).

- **It is called the message of the Lord** – "The Lord's message rang out from you not only in Macedonia and Achaia" (1 The 1:8); "pray for us that the message of the Lord may spread rapidly and be honoured,"

- **The word of the LORD came to the prophets** – "Then the word of the LORD came to Samuel" (1 Sam 15:10); "The words of Jeremiah ... The word of the LORD came to him in ... the reign of Josiah " (Jer 1:1,2).

- **Paul claimed to speak by the Holy Spirit** – "This is what we speak, not in words taught us by human wisdom but in words taught by the Spirit, explaining spiritual realities with Spirit-taught words." (1 Cor 2:13).

- **Peter says of the OT prophets** – "but prophets, though human, spoke from God as they were carried along by the Holy Spirit." (2 Pet 1:21).

- **The word of the apostles is said to be on the same level as the Old Testament prophets** - "I want you to recall the words spoken in the past by the holy prophets and the command given by our Lord and Saviour through your apostles." (2 Pet 3:2).

- **Peter says that Paul's teaching was the same as scripture** – "Paul also wrote you with the wisdom that God gave him. He writes the same way in all his letters, speaking in them of these matters ... which ignorant and unstable people distort, as they do the other Scriptures, to their own destruction." (2 Pet 3:16).

It is interesting to note that the phrases, 'The Lord said' or 'The Lord spoke' or 'The word of the Lord came' are used over 3,800 times in the Bible.

The authority of the Bible

We say that the Bible is unique among all the literature of the world. Can we trust this ancient book as a true record and revelation of God, and his purpose? The first thing we have done is to look at what the Bible says about itself. The Bible claims to be 'the Word of God' a book inspired by God. We should not be afraid of the sceptics accusation that we are arguing around in a circle. In other words, we begin by saying that the Bible is the Word of God. We then say, that the Bible says it is the Word of God, therefore 'it is the Word of God'. We are speaking from a position of faith. We believe firstly, that the Bible recommends itself to us. It does this in the way that it promotes moral goodness and righteousness of character. Secondly, it has proved itself to be reliable and true in our experience. Its promises prove to be true when taken and applied to life in faith. Thirdly, we believe that the Holy Spirit gives us his own witness upon our spirit, concerning the trustworthiness of the Scriptures. Since it is God's very word, then to disbelieve or disobey the Scriptures is to disbelieve or disobey God.

Not every statement in the Bible is true. It contains a record of people speaking lies and false philosophies, such as Job's comforters or parts of Ecclesiastes. There is no revelation, or self disclosure, of God in such statements. However, the whole Bible is put together in such a way that it reveals both good and evil for what they are. It comes together as a complete book that is inspired in all its parts. We agree with Paul when he says that Scripture is to be used to establish all doctrine, and behaviour, in the church, "and is useful for teaching, rebuking, correcting and training in righteousness," (2 Tim 3:16). We as Christians are, "built on the foundation of the apostles and prophets, with Christ Jesus himself as the chief cornerstone." (Eph. 2:20). We do not regard as authoritative any revelation that has been given since the making of the New Testament canon. Nor do we accept the teaching of any person or church as being divinely inspired or authoritative, in the sense that Scripture is. We look to the Scriptures to gain an understanding of all truth regarding God, his purpose in creation and the way of salvation.

✎ Assignment
How should the truth of the authority of Scripture affect our lives?

The New Testament use of the Old Testament

The writers of the New Testament quote the Old Testament over and over and recognise it as the word of God. The Christians, at prayer in Acts, quoted Psalm 2 saying, "You spoke by the Holy Spirit through the mouth of your servant, our father David: 'Why do the nations rage and the peoples plot in vain'?" (Act 4:25-26). Again, Paul quoted from the Psalms (Psa 16:10) in Acts and says, "So it is also stated elsewhere: 'You will not let your holy one see decay.'" (Act 13:35). The letter to the Hebrews uses similar language over and over (Heb 1:5-14). The same letter uses the phrase, "So, as the Holy Spirit says: 'Today, if you hear his voice'" (Heb 3:7), putting it into the present tense, when quoting from the Old Testament. The writer is telling us that the God, who spoke a word in the past, is still speaking it by the Spirit.

We should also note what Jesus said about the Old Testament, as he constantly referred to it in his teaching. In Matthew's gospel Jesus said that not one tiny bit of the law would pass away until all is fulfilled (Mat 5:17-18). Jesus regarded the whole of the Old Testament as a prophetic word that must be fulfilled in himself, "You study the Scriptures diligently because you think that in them you have eternal life. These are the very Scriptures that testify about me," (Jn. 5:39, see also Lk. 4:17-21). He showed his absolute confidence in the OT Scriptures when he spoke to the Jewish leaders and said, "and Scripture cannot be set aside" (Jhn 10:35-36). Jesus believed in the historic accuracy of the Old Testament. He spoke of men like Job, Jonah, Moses and David etc. as real people who were part of God's purpose.

The prophetic nature of Scripture

The Bible is not just a collection of objective truths. In its very nature it is a prophetic book that speaks truth and life to every generation. Because it is 'God-breathed' it carries in its make-up a revelation of God and his unique purpose. From the account of creation in Genesis we learn that the universe came into being by the Word of God, "And God said, 'Let there be' ..." (Gen 1:3,6,9,11). All matter, and every form of life has a peculiar relationship with the Word of God, because it came into being through it. Thus, when Adam and Eve disobeyed the command of God they brought rebellion and disorder into the whole of creation. God intervened by speaking a prophetic word that was to affect the whole of life on this planet "And I will put enmity between you and the woman, and between your offspring and hers; he will crush your head, and you will strike his heel." (Gen 3:15).

The whole flow of human history, as portrayed in the Bible, is about the fulfilment of that prophetic Word of God. Abraham, through his obedience to God's word, became a prophetic figure "By faith Abraham, when called to go to a place he would later receive as his inheritance, obeyed and went, even though he did not know where he was going." (Heb 11:8), (He is called a prophet Gen 20:7). Moses, through his obedience to the Word of God, became a reflection of the prophetic purpose of God "Since then, no prophet has risen in Israel like Moses, whom the LORD knew face to face," (Deu 34:10). The Old Testament prophets carried the directive and creative Word of God to bring about his purpose "Surely the Sovereign LORD does nothing without revealing his plan to his servants the prophets." (Amo 3:7).

For God's ultimate purpose to be fulfilled the Eternal Word of God had to become flesh, (Jhn 1:14) and step into creation in order to show his absolute obedience to the will of God "he humbled himself by becoming obedient to death - even death on a cross!" (Phi 2:8). It was only through this means that mankind could know the restoring power of Redemption, and the whole created order be brought back into complete harmony with the Word of God. The Bible is the record of that Prophetic Word that reveals the heart of God for humanity, and the destiny of the world under the Lordship of Christ, who is the Word of God "His eyes are like blazing fire, and on his head are many crowns ... and his name is the Word of God." (Rev 19:12-13).

Conclusion

We acknowledge that you cannot scientifically prove that the Bible is divinely inspired. But for Christians who are enlightened by the Holy Spirit there is no doubt that this book is the very word of God for every generation. Christians should automatically have a high regard for Scripture since it was through the Scriptures that they heard the gospel, "Consequently, faith comes from hearing the message, and the message is heard through the word about Christ." (Rom 10:17). They were 'born again' through that word, "For you have been born again, not of perishable seed, but of imperishable, through the living and enduring word of God." (1 Pet

1:23). So much of its historic facts have been proved through archaeology, and so many of its prophecies have come to pass, that the book recommends itself. Therefore, the Bible is regarded by Christians as the final court of appeal to establish all practice and doctrine.

"We may be moved and induced by the testimony of the Church to a high and reverend esteem of the holy Scripture, and the heavenliness of the matter, the efficacy of the doctrine, the majesty of the style, the consent of all the parts, the scope of the whole, (which is to give glory to God), the full discovery it makes of the only way of man's salvation, the many other incomparable excellences, and the entire perfection thereof, are arguments by which it gives abundant evidence of itself to be the word of God; yet, notwithstanding, our full persuasion and assurance of the infallible truth, and divine authority of it, is from the inward work of the Holy Spirit, bearing witness by and with the word in our hearts."

- Westminster Confession of Faith ch.1:V

The words of the Bible are not just true in the sense that other books can be true. The Bible is a body of truth and is the measure by which we test all other supposed truths. The Bible is not a text book on science, nor does it claim to tell us everything about every subject. When new scientific or historical facts are proposed, they may cause us to look again at our interpretation of Scripture. Nevertheless, if they clearly contradict the truth of Scripture, we should reject the science as wrong.

The truth of Scripture will stand and God will vindicate it in the end.

Bible Interpretation

Need of Interpretation

Why do we need to interpret the Bible? We believe that it is God's Word for us today. We even have the author of the book, the Holy Spirit, to be our helper and teacher. What more could we possibly need? We should thankfully acknowledge that the Bible has clarity in its message. The sincere seeker, even without special aids, can gather a great deal of truth from it. The Bible is not written in a coded way so that only certain people can understand it. We acknowledge that many parts of the Bible are so clear, that our problem is not understanding the text, but obeying it in practice.

The purpose of biblical interpretation is to make the meaning of various passages of scripture plain to the reader. It should help us evaluate the importance of particular scriptures, and understand what our response to them should be.

Types of literature found in the Bible

- **Narratives** — 1 Samuel, Acts
- **Genealogies** — 1 Chronicles
- **Various laws** — Deuteronomy
- **Poetry** — Psalms
- **Prophecy** — Isaiah, Jeremiah
- **Proverbial sayings** — Proverbs
- **Biographies** — Abraham, Joseph
- **Drama** — Ezekiel ch. 4
- **Parables** — Gospels
- **Letters** — Philippians, Ephesians
- **Sermons** — Acts 2
- **Imagery** — Ezekiel ch. 1
- **Apocalypse** — Daniel, Revelation

Whilst we believe that all Scripture is inspired of God it is important to recognise the different genres of literature found in the Bible. Understanding those genres will affect the way we approach the different writings. The psalms are written in poetic style which calls for a certain licence in their language. David sometimes depicts mountains as 'leaping', and trees 'clapping their hands', in praise to God. The prophets often make use of unusual imagery to communicate their message. Zechariah saw a lamp-stand and olive trees, whilst Jeremiah saw baskets of figs. The letters of Paul contain a great deal of propositional truth, with an exact use of words. All these factors should be taken into consideration when seeking to understand the Bible as God's word for us today.

Different Views

The need of good Bible interpretation becomes evident when we consider the number of cults all claiming to have 'the truth of the Bible'. The Jehovah Witnesses deny the deity of Christ, and the personality of the Holy Spirit, on the basis of the supposed plain truth of scripture. By appealing to a verse from the gospels some N. American sects handle poisonous snakes in order to prove themselves Christians. Even in main stream Christianity there is divergent opinion on matters such as 'eternal security', 'the place of women in the church', 'whether the gifts of the Spirit are for today' and 'church government' etc. All appeal to the same Bible, but their interpretations differs.

Asking the right question

When we are reading any passage of scripture we need to ask two basic questions:

1. What did the writer intend the passage to mean to his readers?
2. What does it mean to us today?

In order to gain a proper appreciation of the verse, chapter or book we need to know the following:

a) To whom was it written?

b) What were the particular circumstances involved?

c) What type of literature was used to convey the truth?

Where do we start?

We readily accept that the language of scripture is not always to be taken literally. We are aware that when Jesus said, "I am the true vine" or "I am the door" his words were not to be interpreted to mean physical objects. By understanding that these words are metaphors, we are applying the simple principle of interpretation to these texts. What about such terms and sayings as "a Sabbath day's journey", "high places", "a denarius"? It is helpful to know the meaning of such terms in order to understand the context in which they are used.

Historic Setting

In order to enhance our understanding of any section of scripture we need to find out some information about it. We need to know the approximate date of the writing and a little of the culture of the people to whom it was sent. Knowledge of the geographical setting and local circumstances may help us further. We also need to find out something of the political factors, and social events of the time. If we do not understand something of the culture of the people to whom it was written we can easily try to apply it direct to our culture, with disastrous results.

The background events to the books of Amos, Hosea or Isaiah will help us understand the burden and content of the prophetic word. The letters Paul wrote to Corinth or Philippi would be better understood if we gathered information about the times and the cities. For some books it is essential to gather such information together. Without some knowledge of the circumstances in Corinth we could easily misread sections of it.

Reading in a context

Some have erred from the truth of scripture by taking verses out of their context. Each sentence must be related to what was said before it, and after it. Every statement must be seen to be a part of the bigger truth that the particular book is teaching. The same goes for the meaning of words. It is not sufficient to merely look up a Bible Concordance to find the meaning of a word. The way the Bible writer uses a word may differ from the secular use of that word. The context will often determine the force or meaning we are to give to a word or a verse.

Problem Texts in the Bible

It is acknowledged that there are a small number of Scripture verses that seem to contradict other Scripture references. Because of this, some have dismissed the Bible as an unreliable book that is full of mistakes. However, most of these seeming errors can be answered quite simply. The few difficulties that remain are probably due to copyist errors. We are not arguing for the infallibility of any translation, but the infallibility of the original manuscripts. It is worth looking at some examples of these problem texts which are given in Appendix 1.

Conclusion

We acknowledge the need for preparatory work, and receiving help from Bible teachers, when doing Bible Study. However, we should always remember that the God of the Bible has given us an extraordinary revelation in the Scriptures. Even for those who do not have the help of good commentaries etc. God can, and does, open up the glory of His Word. When we, with humble heart, look to the Holy Spirit for guidance, we will always come away refreshed and enlightened from studying the Bible.

✎ Assignment
Why is it necessary for the Bible to be the basis of our faith?

Notes

God's Eternal Purpose

Study 2

The Doctrine of God

📖 **Isaiah 40:12-31**

Introduction

Why the study of God? Since we believe in God, and have no query on the matter, isn't that enough? The view that we have of God is of great importance to us. It is a true saying that no people ever rise above their religion, and no religion ever rises above its thoughts of God. If you could assess what an individual thinks of God you could predict the spiritual future of that person. Similarly, look at what the main Christian leaders believe about God and you can foresee the future of the Church.

"That our idea of God corresponds as nearly as possible to the true being of God is of immense importance to us. Compared with our actual thoughts about him, our creedal statements are of little consequence. Our real idea about God may lie buried under the rubbish of conventional religious notions and may require an intelligent and vigorous search before it is finally unearthed and exposed for what it is. Only after an ordeal of painful self-probing are we likely to discover what we actually believe about God."

- Tozer 'The Knowledge of the Holy' p.10

A view that has affected Christians in some circles recently, is the view of God as a 'utilitarian God'. That is, God exists for our benefit, and he dances about to our whims and fancies. People with such views will be taken up with satisfying themselves, and have little time for worshipping, the majesty of God. We should praise God for what he has done, "All your works praise you, LORD; your faithful people extol you." (Psa 145:10). We should worship God for what he is in himself, "Worship the LORD in the splendour of his holiness; tremble before him, all the earth." (Psa 96:9).

✏ **Assignment**

Compare your thoughts about God before you knew Christ with your thoughts of God since coming to Christ.

Where do we start?

How can we begin the study of God? Is it possible to understand anything of the true nature of God? The fallen state of mankind has affected the whole of our nature. It has darkened our minds, dulled our senses, and taken away the true desire to know God (Rom 1:21-23).

"A god begotten in the shadows of a fallen heart will quite naturally be no true likeness of the true God. 'Thou thoughtest,' said the Lord to the wicked man in the psalm, 'that I was altogether such an one as thyself.' Surely this must be a serious affront to the Most High God before whom cherubim and seraphim continually do cry, 'Holy, holy, holy, Lord God of Hosts'."
- Tozer "The Knowledge of the Holy" p.10

The question of Zophar to Job is a relevant one, "Can you fathom the mysteries of God? Can you probe the limits of the Almighty? They are higher than the heavens above--what can you do? They are deeper than the depths below--what can you know?" (Job 11:7-9). The answer is no, we cannot search out these things because the natural mind cannot grasp the mystery of God.

The majesty and glory of God is too great for us to understand, but God has revealed himself to us.

The majesty and glory of God is too great for us to understand, but God has revealed himself to us. Through God dealing with the sin that blinded us, our minds have been opened to know the things that are freely given to us from God. Our spirit is quickened to new life and we begin to understand something of the true nature of God, As the Scripture says, "This is what we speak, not in words taught us by human wisdom but in words taught by the Spirit, explaining spiritual realities with Spirit-taught words." (1 Cor 2:13-14). The very desire in us to know the unknowable God is a sign that we were made in God's image. Something in us cries out to know the source of that image, the God who made us like himself.

The existence of God

The Bible starts with God, "In the beginning God" (Gen 1:1). Here is the foundational doctrine of the Bible – the doctrine of God. Nowhere does the Bible argue about the existence of God. It simply declares it as a fact. Some seek to establish a logical basis to our belief in God. However, we acknowledge that logic has only a limited value in looking into this matter.

Logical Arguments

1. God's existence is shown from the fact of creation – every effect must have a cause, therefore creation must have been established by a creator.

2. God's existence is shown from design – that there is such intricate pattern and order in nature, from the vast solar systems, down to the minute structure of atoms, shows that a great mind must have designed it.

3. God's existence is shown from the moral nature of mankind – seeing that people everywhere have some knowledge of good and evil, it follows that this attribute of conscience must have come from a supreme moral being.

4. God's existence is shown by the universality of religion – because mankind, in every culture across the globe, seek to worship some god, it follows that a god must exist.

Whilst none of these things prove the existence of God in a scientific way, some things just make more sense if there is a God.

1. It is a bigger leap of faith to say 'there is no God' than to say 'there is a God', when we consider how small we are, and the limits of our knowledge. It is an insult to serious thought to adamantly say 'there is no God'. As the psalmist says, "The fool says in his heart, 'There is no God'," (Psa 14:1).

2. The marvellous complexity and fine tuning of the universe does not prove that a great designer planned and made it all. Nonetheless, it makes more sense of the universe to say that a master creator is at the back of it all, than to say that it came from nothing.

3. Human conscience that calls for human rights and care of the weak are not part of a world without God. Evolution demands that the strong eats the weak, because it is the strongest that survive. But human rights and conscience call us to care for the weakest. Where does that come from? It only makes sense if we are made in the image of a compassionate God, who cares for the weak.

The scientist, Professor Richard Dawkins, tries to rationalise religion by speaking of the possibility of a 'god gene' in the human genome. In evolutionary terms, this is supposed to cause us to think of some power superior to ourselves. The truth is, it is not just a single part of the genetic code that makes us think about God, it is that every part of our nature was made to reflect the image of God.

"If there is a God, he must be altogether more mysterious, and far greater than any theologian has ever described."

- Richard Dawkins

I whole heartedly agree with this statement, but such a God does exist. To the questioning heart God has given some answers. He has not answered all the questions, but has revealed enough to satisfy the intellect and capture the heart of those who are open to him.

We should note that God has used several ways to reveal himself.

1. He reveals himself through his creation.
2. He reveals himself through Providence, in history, especially through Israel.
3. He reveals himself through his names.
4. He reveals himself through his attributes.
5. He reveals himself through his Son.

In this study we will concentrate more on the way that God has revealed himself through his names and through his attributes. In a later study we will look at how God reveals himself in the fullest sense through His Son.

God is Person

God is not an abstract force or nameless power - he is real person. A person is a moral being with mind, intelligence, will, individuality, self-consciousness and self determination, and the Bible reveals such a God. It reveals a God who plans all things, "the plan of him who works out everything in conformity with the purpose of his will," (Eph 1:11). It reveals a God who converses with men and builds a relationship with them. He did this with Adam, "But the LORD God called to the man, "Where are you?" (Gen 3:9). He also did this with Abraham, "The LORD had said to Abram, "Go from your country, your people and your father's household to the land I will show you." (Gen 12:1). Last of all, God revealed himself through 'the man Christ Jesus', "The Word became flesh and made his dwelling among us. We have seen his glory, the glory of the one and only Son, who came from the Father, full of grace and truth" (Jhn 1:14).

Assignment
In which ways does God speak to us today?

The Names of God

God has revealed something of the truth about his nature, by giving us special names for himself. In Scripture a name is often used to reveal someone's character, and this is seen in the names of God given to us in the Scriptures, especially in the divine name Yahweh. The name of God is to be revered and not used flippantly, "You shall not misuse the name of the LORD your God, for the LORD will not hold anyone guiltless who misuses his name." (Exo 20:7).

Note that in Scripture translations:

Lord = sovereign one, **LORD** = Yahweh.

God = Sovereign one, **GOD** = Yahweh.

The Hebrew words used in the Bible for God:-

El – It denotes a supreme one, a lord and carries the idea of strength and power. It is the masculine noun, singular which is used about 240 times in the Old Testament. It is mainly translated as God, but also occasionally as god (meaning foreign god). It is occasionally translated to speak of men in high position or mighty warriors.

Elohim – This word is used over 2600 times in the Old Testament. It is the masculine, plural form of 'El', and it emphasises the strength and power of the God who is to be feared. It may also be the beginning of the revelation, that the God who is one being, is also three persons. It is almost always translated as God but occasionally as gods or angels.

Elyon – Meaning elevated one, denoting the exalted position of God.

Adonai – The masculine singular noun used exclusively of God (used well over 400 times in the Old Testament). It is translated as Lord and is used by the Jewish people in place of the name Yahweh. It points to the supreme authority and power of God.

Shaddai – It shows God as all powerful, and one who is the source of all blessing.

Yahweh

This is the great name of God. It's basic meaning is 'I am who I am' or 'I shall be what I shall be' (Exo 3:14). It reveals God as the unchangeable and self existent one. This is God's covenant name by which he commits himself to those who trust him.

The name 'Yahweh' is often linked with descriptive words to reveal the God who meets his people in different situations of life. The following names begin to open our understanding to the nature of God and his care for his people:

Yahweh-jireh – Yahweh Provider "So Abraham called that place The LORD Will Provide" (Gen 22:14).

Yahweh-ropheh – Yahweh who heals "I will not bring on you any of the diseases I brought on the Egyptians, for I am the LORD, who heals you" (Exo 15:26).

Yahweh-sabaoth – Yahweh of the hosts of angels, "and they brought back the ark of the covenant of the LORD Almighty, who is enthroned between the cherubim" (1 Sam 4:4).

Yahweh-shalom - Yahweh our peace, "So Gideon built an altar to the LORD there and called it The LORD Is Peace." (Jdg 6:24)

Yahweh-nissi – Yahweh our banner, "Moses built an altar and called it The LORD is my Banner." (Exo 17:15).

Yahweh-ro'eh – Yahweh my Shepherd, "The LORD is my shepherd, I lack nothing." (Psa 23:1).

Yahweh-tsidkenu – Yahweh our righteousness, "This is the name by which he will be called: The LORD Our Righteous Saviour." (Jer 23:6).

Yahweh-shammah – Yahweh who is present, "And the name of the city from that time on will be: THE LORD IS THERE." (Eze 48:35).

Yahweh-maccaddashem – Yahweh your sanctifier, "so you may know that I am the LORD, who makes you holy." (Exo 31:13).

Yahweh-Yeshua – Not used in Scripture but, is the ultimate revelation of God in Jesus Christ. He says to the Father, "I have revealed you [your name] to those whom you gave me out of the world" (Jhn 17:6)

The attributes of God

The scripture reveals something of the glory of God. These divinely revealed aspects of glory and perfection are called 'attributes'. Although we divide up these attributes, in order to understand them, we should remember that God himself is not divided into parts. He is one glorious, united divine being. An attribute of God is essentially whatever God has revealed about himself.

The incommunicable attributes of God

God is beyond human comprehension. This is because there are attributes of God which he cannot share with any other. They are the very things that make him to be God, "Great is the LORD and most worthy of praise; his greatness no one can fathom." (Psa 145:3). Paul speaks of the absolute personality of God, "God, the blessed and only Ruler, the King of kings and Lord of lords, who alone is immortal and who lives in unapproachable light, whom no one has seen or can see. To him be honour and might forever. Amen." (1 Tim 6:16).

a) **God is eternal** – God is infinite in regard to time. We can only think within time, and measure a succession of moments. Even when thinking of eternity we tend to look backwards, then forwards. But God lives within an eternal now. "Before the mountains were born or you brought forth the whole world, from everlasting to everlasting you are God." (Psa 90:2). Isaiah cried out, "Do you not know? Have you not heard? The LORD is the everlasting God, the Creator of the ends of the earth." (Isa 40:28). Peter calls us to be patient in life in view of God's eternity, "But do not forget this one thing, dear friends: With the Lord a day is like a thousand years, and a thousand years are like a day." (2 Pet 3:8). This eternal God created the sphere of time and works in it to accomplish his purpose.

b) **God is self-existent** – We understand only cause and effect. Everything we see must have been caused by something, until we come to God, the original cause of all. God has no origin, he is the beginning of all beginnings, "In the beginning God" (Gen 1:1); "In the beginning was the Word" (Jhn 1:1).

c) **God is self-sufficient** – There is no deficiency in God, for everything he needs is in himself. All creatures are dependant upon support from outside themselves for their well being. God is not dependant on anything outside of himself, he is "Yahweh, - I am, that I am". Isaiah catches a glimpse of him as the only one "Who has measured the waters in the hollow of his hand, or with the breadth of his hand marked off the heavens? Who has held the dust of the earth in a basket, or weighed the mountains on the scales and the hills in a balance?" (Isa. 40:12-17); "Do you not know? Have you not heard? The LORD is the everlasting God, the Creator of the ends of the earth. He will not grow tired or weary, and his understanding no one can fathom" (Isa. 40:28).

d) **God is immutable** – It is impossible for God to change because he is already in a state of absolute perfection. He is everlastingly the same. The scripture speaks of changes in God's actions. He is said to 'come' and 'go'; 'hiding' and 'revealing' himself. He is also said to 'repent', "I will wipe from the face of the earth the human race I have created ... for I regret that I have made them" (Gen 6:7). Nevertheless, there is no essential change in God's character and being, as the prophet makes clear, "I the LORD do not change." (Mal 3:6). James caught a glimpse of this attribute of God and wrote, "Every good and perfect gift is from above, coming down from the Father of the heavenly lights, who does not change like shifting shadows." (Jam 1:17). God is unchangeable in his essential being, his character and his purpose.

e) **God is omniscient** – God has perfect and complete knowledge of all things. God does not reason out knowledge, he is all-knowing. He never adds to his knowledge because all possibilities of knowledge are in him. Job asks the question, "Can anyone teach knowledge to God, since he judges even the highest?" (Job 21:22). Isaiah, in a similar way questions all those who would doubt the enormity of God's understanding, "Whom did the LORD consult to enlighten him, and who taught him the right way? Who was it that taught him knowledge, or showed him the path of understanding?" (Isa 40:13,14). The answer is that no one can add to God's knowledge in any way. As human beings we are particularly interested in his complete knowledge of us, see the whole of Psalm 139, "You have searched me, LORD, and you know me. You know when I sit and when I rise; you perceive my thoughts from afar." (Psa 139:1,2).

f) **God is omnipresent** – God is infinite in regard to space. There is no spatial dimension to God. He is present everywhere, in all his fullness. God is said to dwell in heaven - it is his throne. He is especially there in the sense that he manifests the fullness of his glory there. However, he does not reveal his fullness in all places. In one place he reveals his gracious presence; in another he reveals his judgements as a consuming fire. Solomon, after building the temple, came to understand that God could not confine his presence to one place, "But will God really dwell on earth? The heavens, even the highest heaven, cannot contain you. How much less this temple I have built!" (1 Kgs 8:27). Jeremiah, as a spokesman for God raises the question, "'Am I only a God nearby,' declares the LORD, 'and not a God far away? Who can hide in secret places so that I cannot see them?' declares the LORD. 'Do not I fill heaven and earth?' declares the LORD" (Jer 23:23,24).

g) **God is omnipotent** – It is this attribute that enables God to bring to pass everything that he wills, without hindrance. He has endless, boundless power and authority over all realms. "For since the creation of the world God's invisible qualities--his eternal power and divine nature have been clearly seen" (Rom 1:20); "Yours, LORD, is the greatness and the power and the glory and the majesty and the splendour, for everything in heaven and earth is yours. Yours, LORD, is the kingdom; you are exalted as head over all." (1 Chr 29:11). God's sovereign will covers all things in heaven and earth, past, present and future. That will and power of God is expressed in creation, providence and salvation.

h) **God is Spirit** – "God is spirit, and his worshippers must worship in the Spirit and in truth" (Jhn 4:24). Spirit is the very substance of his being. We only understand matter in a three dimensional world as we see, hear, touch, taste, and smell. Through those senses we assess and relate to everything around us. But what is pure, original, uncreated Spirit? - That is God. Because he is spirit, God is one pure, indivisible substance.

✎ Assignment
What should these glorious attributes of God inspire in us?

The communicable attributes of God

There are attributes that reveal the personal and moral nature of God. In them he shows the glory of his character. These attributes are shared with his moral creatures - God can be known in a personal way.

The Scripture speaks of God as one who can be known in an intimate way, "A father to the fatherless, a defender of widows, is God in his holy dwelling." (Psa 68:5); "The LORD watches over the foreigner and sustains the fatherless and the widow" (Psa146:9). He is spoken of as one who is mindful of the downtrodden and weary and the one who comes to the aid of those in trouble.

a) **Holiness** – Here is the moral excellence of God, for he is incapable of sinning. God does not live to a standard of holiness outside of himself, he is that standard, "Who among the gods is like you, LORD? Who is like you-- majestic in holiness, awesome in glory, working wonders?" (Exo 15:11). From his own holy nature he calls us as his people to be holy, "But just as he who called you is holy, so be holy in all you do; for it is written: "Be holy, because I am holy." (1 Pet 1:15-16). God's holiness is so high that it sets him apart from all his creation - He is other. His holiness is coextensive with himself. It governs all that he is and does. So, God is holy in his mercy and his love, as well as in his judgement and wrath. Thus, holiness is his first attribute. Everything directly associated with God in the Bible becomes holy, the tabernacle, the temple, heaven, Sabbath, Zion and then his people.

b) **Faithfulness** – The God 'whose word is his bond', never changes in his moral character, and always fulfils his promises, "God did this so that, by two unchangeable things in which it is impossible for God to lie, we ... may be greatly encouraged." (Heb 6:18). Paul wrote of this quality of God and said, "if we are faithless, he remains faithful, for he cannot disown himself." (2 Tim 2:13).

c) **Goodness** – This is the kindness of God that always seeks the good of his creation, "How priceless is your unfailing love, O God! People take refuge in the shadow of your wings." (Psa 36:7). The psalmist again says, "How abundant are the good things that you have stored up for those who fear you, that you bestow in the sight of all, on those who take refuge in you." (Psa 31:19). Paul saw the goodness of God as the motivating drive in his dealings with us, "Or do you show contempt for the riches of his kindness, forbearance and patience, not realizing that God's kindness is intended to lead you to repentance?" (Rom 2:4).

d) **Justice** – The righteous character of God causes him to judge all things uprightly, without bias or prejudice, "Righteousness and justice are the foundation of your throne; love and faithfulness go before you." (Psa 89:14). "And there is no God apart from me, a righteous God and a Saviour; there is none but me." (Isa 45:21); "For the LORD is righteous, he loves justice; the upright will see his face" (Psa 11:7).

The justice of God is directly linked with the wrath of God. Some people find it difficult to think of God in terms of wrath but the Bible has much to say about it. "Remember this and never forget how you aroused the anger of the LORD your God in the wilderness... At Horeb you aroused the LORD's wrath so that he was angry enough to destroy you." (Deu 9:7-8). The New Testament also raises this aspect of God's character. "Whoever believes in the Son has eternal life, but whoever rejects the Son will not see life, for God's wrath remains on them." (Jhn 3:36). God's wrath is not to be thought of as an uncontrollable emotion, nor as a vindictive element in God. God's wrath is full of holiness and is spoken of along with his patience. "The LORD is compassionate and gracious, slow to anger, abounding in love. He will not always accuse, nor will he harbour his anger forever;" Psa 103:8-9).

e) **Mercy** – This is the divine compassion of God, which is not a temporary frame of mind, but a permanent attribute of the Almighty. Much of the use of the word 'mercy' in the Old Testament translates the Hebrew 'racham' which, in Hebrew idiom, denotes the deep compassion of the womb. David, when in failure, pleaded, "David said to Gad, "I am in deep distress. Let me fall into the hands of the LORD, for his mercy (racham) is very great;" (1 Chr 21:13). The prophet Habakkuk saw how near the judgements of God were and cried, "LORD, I have heard of your fame; I stand in awe of your deeds, LORD. Repeat them in our day, in our time make them known; in wrath remember mercy (racham)." (Hab 3:2). Paul after describing our lost condition cried out, "But because of his great love for us, God, who is rich in mercy," (Eph 2:4).

f) **Love** – This is the attribute that moves God to communicate with us in a special way. The affections of God are set on mankind. In spite of all the evil that has come into the world, the love of God was the prime cause of our existence. It is only the amazing love of God that can bring sense and meaning to life, "For God so loved the world that he gave his one and only Son, that whoever believes in him shall not perish but have eternal life." (Jhn 3:16). It was, "In love he predestined us for adoption to sonship through Jesus Christ, in accordance with his pleasure and will" (Eph. 1:5). John when dealing with the greatness of the love of God says, "Whoever does not love does not know God, because God is love. This is how God showed his love among us: He sent his one and only Son into the world that we might live through him. This is love: not that we loved God, but that he loved us and sent his Son as an atoning sacrifice for our sins." (1 Jhn 4:8-10). This love will triumph over all evil and accomplish God's redemptive purpose for this planet.

g) **Blessedness** – Everything about God is absolute perfection. He has no shortcomings or limitations. He is constantly in a state of eternal, absolute blessedness, "the sound doctrine that conforms to the gospel concerning the glory of the blessed God, which he entrusted to me" (1 Tim 1:11).

The revelation of God to Moses, in the giving of the Ten Commandments, displayed many of these attributes, "And he passed in front of Moses, proclaiming, 'The LORD, the LORD, the compassionate and gracious God, slow to anger, abounding in love and faithfulness, maintaining love to thousands, and forgiving wickedness, rebellion and sin. Yet he does not leave the guilty unpunished; he punishes the children and their children for the sin of the parents to the third and fourth generation.'" (Exo 34:6-7).

All these communicable attributes reveal God's character and, through the work of redemption, he actually renews them in us, "and to put on the new self, created to be like God in true righteousness and holiness." (Eph 4:24). In regard to these attributes of God we are called to " Follow God's example, therefore, as dearly loved children and walk in the way of love," (Eph 5:1-2).

✎ Assignment
How can we rightly speak of a God of love and yet speak of a God of wrath?

God in Unity and Trinity

The truth of Trinity lies at the root of all Christian teaching. If we go wrong here the whole structure of what we believe will be wrong. A right understanding of God in unity and trinity separates Christianity from all other religions.

God in unity

We believe that God is one, for there is only one God. The declaration to Israel long ago was, "Hear, O Israel: The LORD our God, the LORD is one." (Deu 6:4). Christians are sometimes falsely accused of believing in three gods, but God is one indivisible substance, "And there is no God apart from me, a righteous God and a Saviour; there is none but me." (Isa 45:21). As Moses declared, "For the LORD your God is God of gods and Lord of lords, the great God, mighty and awesome," (Deu 10:17).

"The doctrine of the divine unity means not only that there is but one God; it means also that God is simple, uncomplex, one with himself. The harmony of his being is the result not of a perfect balance of parts but of the absence of parts. Between his attributes no contradiction can exist. He need not suspend one to exercise another, for in him all his attributes are one".
 - Tozer 'The Knowledge of the Holy' p.23

God's Eternal Purpose: An introduction to Christian doctrine

God in Trinity

The God, who is one absolute, eternal being, reveals himself as three persons - the Father, the Son, and the Holy Spirit. Each person possesses the fullness of the divine essence and yet remains distinct in person-hood. We should not expect to understand all the deep mysteries involved in this, but we can accept and believe it as the truth of scripture.

> *The God, who is one absolute, eternal being, reveals himself as three persons*

Scripture proof of Trinity

The word 'Trinity' is never used in the Bible, but the truth involved in the word is taught in many places. In the Old Testament God speaks of himself in the plural, "Then God said, "Let us make mankind in our image, in our likeness" (Gen 1:26). The way that the name Yahweh is linked with the plural word for God, 'Elohim' suggests one God in plurality of person, "when the LORD (Yahweh) God (Elohim) made the earth and the heavens." (Gen 2:4).

Even in the Old Testament we are given glimpses of God in three persons. The Son that God would send into the world would be called "Mighty God" (Isa 9:6). The Spirit of God is seen as a separate person from God, "The Spirit of the LORD will rest on him" (Isa 11:2). In the New Testament the doctrine of trinity becomes even clearer.

The Father and the Son – The Bible speaks of God the Father in relation to his only begotten Son, "We have seen his glory, the glory of the one and only Son, who came from the Father, full of grace and truth." (Jhn 1:14). John further teaches, "No one has ever seen God, but the one and only Son, who is himself God and is in closest relationship with the Father, has made him known" (Jhn 1:18).

The Holy Spirit – All the attributes of divine person-hood are present in the Holy Spirit. Jesus promised his disciples that he would send a person, of the same kind as himself, to them, "And I will ask the Father, and he will give you another *(of the same kind)* advocate to help you and be with you forever" (Jhn 14:16).

Three divine persons working together

The Scripture reveals the three persons of Godhead working in unity, yet they have particular ministries within that unity. All are involved in the work of creation and redemption, but there is an order and emphasis in what they do. The Father acts through the Son, by the Holy Spirit.

The Father – planned the work of creation and redemption. He was the inspiration and power behind all things, "he made known to us the mystery of his will according to his good pleasure, which he purposed in Christ," (Eph 1:9).

The Son – mediated the work of creation. It was all brought about through him, "For in him all things were created: things in heaven and on earth, visible and invisible, whether thrones or powers or rulers or authorities; all things have been created through him and for him." (Col 1:16). In the same way the whole work of redemption was brought about through the Son, "All this is from God, who reconciled us to himself through Christ" (2 Cor 5:18,19).

The Spirit – finished the work of creation. It was by his power that all things were completed, "and the Spirit of God was hovering over the waters." (Gen 1:2), and " By his breath *(Spirit)* the skies became fair;" (Job 26:13).

The truth of Trinity is deeply embedded in Scripture as an essential truth regarding the self-revelation of God. There are many Scriptures that refer to the three divine persons working together e.g.:

In the baptism of Christ, **Jesus** is seen standing in the water, the **Holy Spirit** comes upon him and the **Father** speaks from heaven (Mat 3:16). Believers are to be baptised, "in the name of the **Father** and of the **Son** and of the **Holy Spirit**," (Mat 28:19). Paul commends his readers to the whole trinity "May the grace of the **Lord Jesus Christ**, and the love of **God**, and the fellowship of the **Holy Spirit** be with you all." (2 Cor 13:14). Jude, too, brings them together, "praying in the **Holy Spirit**, keep yourselves in **God's** love as you wait for the mercy of our **Lord Jesus Christ** to bring you to eternal life." (Jud 1:20-21).

Conclusion

No religion on earth has a revelation of God like the God of the Bible. The peoples of the earth have worshipped many gods, "But their idols are silver and gold, made by human hands. They have mouths, but cannot speak, eyes, but cannot see" (Psa 115:5). The Koran gives some insights into the nature of God, partly based on the OT, but you are left with a harsh, mechanical, unfeeling God who is quite unlike the God of the Bible.

The God who is revealed to us through the Holy Scripture is to be worshipped as the only true and living God.

✎ Assignment
Why is it important to believe and teach the doctrine of Trinity?

Notes

God's Eternal Purpose

Study 3
The Doctrine of Christ

📖 **Philippians 2:1-11**

Introduction

The person of Jesus Christ stands at the centre of the Christian faith. Unlike all other religions, Christianity could not exist without its founder. If the founder of another religion had never existed, someone else could have taken his place. In the case of Jesus Christ, he is not only the founder of Christianity, he is its life and substance. What we believe about him is of great importance. When Jesus asked his disciples, "Who do people say I am?", he put forward a question that was to occupy the minds of many in every succeeding generation. The answer to that question has altered the course of many lives, families, and even nations. The early disciples firstly saw him as a man - the Messiah, but later they came to understand that he was God come in human nature.

Jesus asked "Who do people say I am?"

Most of the heresies that the church has had to deal with over the centuries have been about the person of Jesus Christ. Some have denied his true God-hood, while others have denied his true human nature. These heresies, in one form or another, have persisted unto this day.

Martin Lloyd-Jones gives this warning:

"It was because such simple Christians were ready to believe false teachers, and, indeed, did believe them, that so many of the epistles had to be written, with the stern warnings against the terrible danger to the soul of believing these wrong teachings and false ideas concerning our Lord and Saviour Jesus Christ".

- Lloyd-Jones 'Great Doctrines Series - Vol.1' p.247

Old Testament predictions

Jesus was a Jew by birth and life, confining almost all his ministry within the borders of that small nation. So it is to that nation we should look first for a guide as to who Jesus is. God called Israel into a close relationship with himself, (Deu 4:34,35). It was to this nation that God promised to send one who would fulfil his purpose.

- **Jacob spoke of the coming of a great ruler,** "The sceptre will not depart from Judah, nor the ruler's staff from between his feet, until he to whom it belongs shall come and the obedience of the nations shall be his." (Gen 49:10).
- **Moses predicted the coming of a special prophet,** "The LORD said to me ... I will raise up for them a prophet like you from among their fellow Israelites, and I will put my words in his mouth. He will tell them everything I command him." (Deu 18:17-18).
- **Baalim saw a star coming out of Jacob,** "A star will come out of Jacob; a sceptre will rise out of Israel." (Num 24:17).
- **David anticipated the coming of a chosen king,** "I have installed my king on Zion, my holy mountain. I will proclaim the LORD's decree: He said to me, 'You are my son; today I have become your father'." (Psa 2:6,7).
- **David also saw a priest coming from another order,** "The LORD has sworn and will not relent, you are a priest forever according to the order of Melchizedek" (Psa 110:4).
- **David calls this one 'God',** "Your throne, O God, will last for ever and ever; a sceptre of justice will be the sceptre of your kingdom." (Psa 45:6,7).
- **Isaiah sees one called Immanuel (God with us),** "The virgin will conceive and give birth to a son, and will call him Immanuel." (Isa 7:14).
- **One of the great names bestowed on Messiah would be,** "Mighty God" (Isa 9:6).
- **The servant of Yahweh would die for the sins of the people** (Isa 53)

All these promises were fulfilled in the coming of Jesus Christ into the world. The gospel accounts repeatedly use the statement, "All this took place to fulfil what the Lord had said through the prophet:" (Mat 1:22). Jesus Christ is the one who is at the centre of the eternal purpose of God.

What Jesus said about himself

Although Jesus was reluctant to tell the people in plain terms that he was equal with God the Father, some of his statements regarding himself come very close to it and were understood by his enemies to mean that.

- **He claimed to have an existence before Abraham,** "'Very truly I tell you', Jesus answered, 'before Abraham was born, I am'!" (Jhn 8:58).
- **He claimed to have seen the Father,** "No one has seen the Father except the one who is from God; only he has seen the Father." (Jhn 6:46).
- **He said, that to see him was to see the Father,** "Anyone who has seen me has seen the Father. How can you say, Show us the Father?" (Jhn 14:9)
- **He had the glory of the Father from all eternity,** "And now, Father, glorify me in your presence with the glory I had with you before the world began." (Jhn 17:5).
- **His enemies accused him of making himself equal with God,** "'We are not stoning

you for any good work,' they replied, 'but for blasphemy, because you, a mere man, claim to be God'." (Jhn 10:30-33).

In the light of all this, we must consider that Jesus Christ was either all that he said he was, or he was a fanatic who was completely deluded. There is no middle ground for us to stand on.

We cannot just accept his good moral teaching and example, but reject who he said he was.

✎ Assignment

How important is the person of Jesus Christ in God's plan of Salvation?

The human nature of Christ

The gospel accounts of Jesus present to us a real man living in a real world. The title he repeatedly took for himself and which is mentioned some 77 times in the gospels is, 'The son of man'. Hebrews tells us that he took our human nature for his own, "Since the children have flesh and blood, he too shared in their humanity" (Heb 2:14). Christ accepted all the limitations that human nature imposed upon him. The Son of God was limited by that human body, to being in one place at one time. He was limited in his knowledge of events, and required all the normal means to sustain life.

The virgin birth

Though the human nature of Jesus was like ours, his conception was extraordinary. Mary was with child before she had any intimate relationship with Joseph, "But he did not consummate their marriage until she gave birth to a son." (Mat 1:25). Nor had she had sexual relationship with any other man, "'How will this be', Mary asked the angel, 'since I am a virgin?'" (Luk 1:34). It was by the power of the Holy Spirit that Mary conceived and gave birth to a son. The seed of Mary was used, but not the seed of a man. The whole miracle took place by the overshadowing of the Holy Spirit, "The angel answered, 'The Holy Spirit will come on you, and the power of the Most High will overshadow you. So the holy one to be born will be called the Son of God'." (Luk 1:35, see also Mat 1:18).

The human body of Jesus

An early heresy the church encountered was the teaching that the body of Jesus was a mere phantom. Some taught that since all flesh was sinful God could not become incarnate. The apostle John dealt with this issue by saying that any denial of the reality of Christ's physical body, was of the spirit of anti-Christ, "This is how you can recognize the Spirit of God: Every spirit that acknowledges that Jesus Christ has come in the flesh is from God, but every spirit that does not acknowledge Jesus is not from God. This is the spirit of the antichrist, which you have heard is coming" (1 Jhn 4:2-3).

- **His birth was normal,** "and she gave birth to her firstborn, a son. She wrapped him in cloths and placed him in a manger," (Luk 2:7).

- **His age is noted at eight days,** "On the eighth day, when it was time to circumcise the child, he was named Jesus" (Luk 2:21).

- **His age is noted at forty days,** "When the time came for the purification rites required by the Law of Moses, Joseph and Mary took him to Jerusalem to present him to the Lord" (Luk 2:22)
- **His age is noted at twelve years,** "When he was twelve years old, they went up to the festival" (Luk 2:42)
- **He began his public ministry at about thirty years,** "Now Jesus himself was about thirty years old when he began his ministry." (Luk 3:23).
- **He was subject to the normal laws of physical and mental growth,** "And the child grew and became strong; he was filled with wisdom and the grace of God was on him." (Luk 2:40)
- **He ate and drank as a normal man,** "The Son of Man came eating and drinking," (Luk 7:34).
- **He was subject to weariness,** "and Jesus, tired as he was from the journey, sat down by the well. It was about noon." (Jhn 4:6).
- **He suffered physical and emotional pain,** "And being in anguish, he prayed more earnestly, and his sweat was like drops of blood falling to the ground." (Luk 22:44).

The human soul of Jesus

Equally real was the human soul of Christ. The gospels speak of the whole range of human feelings, intelligence and will that make up human soul.

- **He experienced the emotion of joy,** "At that time Jesus, full of joy through the Holy Spirit, said, 'I praise you, Father,'" (Luk 10:21).
- **He showed compassion on the multitudes,** "I have compassion for these people; they have already been with me three days and have nothing to eat." (Mar 8:2).
- **He used natural, discriminating love,** "Now Jesus loved Martha and her sister and Lazarus." (Jhn 11:5).
- **He was angry at the stubbornness of the leaders over Sabbath,** "He looked around at them in anger and, deeply distressed at their stubborn hearts" (Mar 3:5).
- **He exercised a human will,** "For I have come down from heaven not to do my will but to do the will of him who sent me." (Jhn 6:38).
- **He was put under the pressure of temptation,** "Because he himself suffered when he was tempted, he is able to help those who are being tempted." (Heb 2:18).

Christ continues to have a human nature, in the glories of heaven. In his exaltation to the throne of God he has never put aside this vital link with us.

His human body, after the resurrection, may have been changed in its make-up. However, it was still a real human body, "Look at my hands and my feet. It is I myself! Touch me and see, a ghost does not have flesh and bones, as you see I have." (Luk 24:39).

Stephen saw the Christ enthroned in heaven, "But Stephen, full of the Holy Spirit, looked up to heaven and saw the glory of God, and Jesus standing at the right hand of God." (Act 7:55-56) (see also Act 1:9).

His human nature will be seen in the second coming, "But I say to all of you: From now on you will see the Son of Man sitting at the right hand of the Mighty One and coming on the clouds of heaven." (Mat 26:64). The angels witnessed to this, "'Men of Galilee,' ... 'This same Jesus, who has been taken from you into heaven, will come back in the same way you have seen him go into heaven.'"(Act 1:11).

While the New Testament makes clear Christ's closeness to us, it also shows how he stood apart from all other men. He was without sin, "but we have one who has been tempted in every way, just as we are--yet he did not sin." (Heb 4:15). In his absolute purity he could challenge **men**, "Can any of you prove me guilty of sin?" (Jhn 8:46), and could challenge the **devil**, "for the prince of this world is coming. He has no hold over me," (Jhn 14:30). He alone could say in the absolute sense, "I have brought you glory on earth by finishing the work you gave me to do." (Jhn 17:4).

Assignment
In which ways was the Son of God restricted in his coming to earth as a man?

The divine nature of Christ

Was Jesus God? If he was not we should not put our faith in him at all. To say he was a great moral teacher and yet reject his claim to deity makes no sense.

The truth of Christ's deity stands as the cornerstone of the Christian faith.

It has been challenged by heretical groups down through the centuries. However, the scriptures decisively teach, both directly and indirectly, that Jesus Christ is God.

- **Christ The Son of God** – Christ is called 'The Son of God' some forty times in scripture. Five times he is called, 'the one and only Son', which marks his son-ship as unique. Adam was called the son of God because he was created by God, (Luk 3:38). Jesus claimed original, begotten son-ship, making himself equal with God, "For this reason they tried all the more to kill him; not only was he breaking the Sabbath, but he was even calling God his own Father, making himself equal with God." (Jhn 5:18). Paul makes his confession of Christ, "regarding his Son ... and who through the Spirit of holiness was appointed the Son of God in power by his resurrection from the dead:" (Rom 1:2-3). He was also called the son of God because of his position as Messiah King, "Simon Peter answered, 'You are the Messiah, the Son of the living God'." (Mat 16:16); "When the centurion and those with him ... exclaimed, 'Surely he was the Son of God!'" (Mat 27:54).

- **He is called God** – In the most direct statements Christ is recognised as God, "and from them is traced the human ancestry of the Messiah, who is God over all, forever praised! Amen." (Rom 9:5). "while we wait for the blessed hope--the appearing of the glory of our great God and Saviour, Jesus Christ," (Tit 2:13).

- **He is the exact image of God** – Man was made in the image of God and so inherited God likeness, (Gen 1:26). However, the Scripture says of Christ, "The Son is the radiance of God's glory and the exact representation of his being," (Heb 1:3). He is not said to be made in the image of God, but to be that image, "The Son is the image of the invisible God, the firstborn over all creation." (Col 1:15).

- **The fullness of God in Christ** – All that God is in his essential being is found in Christ, "For God was pleased to have all his fullness dwell in him," (Col 1:19). "For in Christ all the fullness of the Deity lives in bodily form," (Col 2:9).

- **He exists in the nature of God** – "Who, being in very nature God, did not consider equality with God something to be used to his own advantage;" (Phi 2:6). This Scripture deals with both the true human nature of Christ and his Divine nature.

- **He has original life in himself** – In the way that the Father is self-existent, the Son of God is the same, "For as the Father has life in himself, so he has granted the Son also to have life in himself." (Jhn 5:26).

- **He is the Word, equal with God** – "In the beginning was the Word, and the Word was with God, and the Word was God." (Jhn 1:1).

- **He is called Lord** – This title in the New Testament is sometimes used as the equivalent of Yahweh, in the Old Testament. It is used of Jesus in this way several times, "announcing the good news of peace through Jesus Christ, who is Lord of all." (Act 10:36); "and every tongue acknowledge that Jesus Christ is Lord, to the glory of God the Father." (Phi 2:11). Linked with this is the use of the divine name "I Am" by Jesus, "before Abraham was born, I Am" (Jhn 8:58).

- **He received worship** – To the Jew it was blasphemy to give or receive worship, except to God alone. Yet it was Jews who gave worship to Jesus, and he accepted it without reserve, "Then those who were in the boat worshipped him, saying, 'Truly you are the Son of God.'" (Mat 14:33); "They came to him, clasped his feet and worshipped him." (Mat 28:9). When God sent his Son into the world he instructed the angels to worship him, "Let all God's angels worship him." (Heb 1:6).

His divine attributes

There are things said of Christ that can only mean that the very attributes of Deity belong to him, in the fullest sense.

- **Omnipotence** – The gospels show that Christ had direct authority over sickness, demons, nature, and death. This authority was not just a temporary thing. After the resurrection, Christ said, "All authority in heaven and on earth has been given to me" (Mat 28:18). Further, the Bible says, of him, "sustaining all things by his powerful word." (Heb 1:3).

- **Omnipresence** – Jesus promised his personal presence to believers to the very end of time, "And surely I am with you always, to the very end of the age." (Mat 28:20). He could never fulfil such a promise unless he was unlimited in his person as to time and space. In this respect Christ "fills everything in every way." (Eph 1:23).

- **Omniscience** – Christ had supernatural insight into the hearts of men, "for he knew all people. He did not need any testimony about mankind, for he knew what was in each person." (Jhn 2:24-25). Beyond that, Paul says of Christ, "in whom are hidden all the treasures of wisdom and knowledge." (Col 2:3).

- **Eternal** – John says of Christ "He was with God in the beginning." (Jhn 1:2). Christ said of himself, "'I am the Alpha and the Omega'," says the Lord God, 'who is, and who was, and who is to come, the Almighty'." (Rev 1:8).

- **He is Creator** – John acknowledged this, "Through him all things were made; without him nothing was made that has been made." (Jhn 1:3). Paul declared the same, "For in him all things were created: things in heaven and on earth, visible and invisible, whether thrones or powers or rulers or authorities; all things have been created through him and for him." (Col 1:16).

Assignment
In which ways can we honour Jesus Christ as Lord?

Two natures in one person

Jesus Christ is truly man and truly God. He has a human nature and a divine nature. This does not make him two persons. He is not a human person and a divine person. Jesus Christ is a divine person who was God from all eternity, but who took human nature as his own, "Who, being in very nature God ... by taking the very nature of a servant, being made in human likeness." (Phi 2:6-7). This is the most amazing truth in the whole Bible – that the Son of God should come into the world as a man and be joined with that human nature forever.

"For Jesus neither laid aside his deity when he came to earth nor his humanity when he returned to heaven."

- John Blanchard

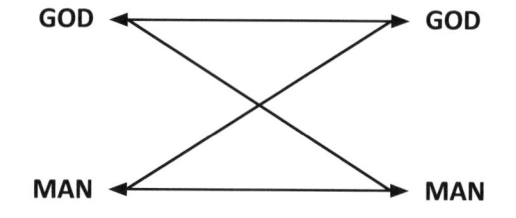

Christ is:

- **God to God** & **Man to Man**
- **Man to God** & **God to Man**

"Notice what I am saying. I am not saying that when Jesus of Nazareth was born in Bethlehem a new personality came into being. That is not true. That is rank heresy. The doctrine of the incarnation says that the eternal second person in the blessed Trinity entered into time and into the world, took unto himself human nature, was born as a babe, lived a life as a man, and appeared in 'the likeness of sinful flesh' (Rom 8:3) ... the one who was born was not coming into being, was not starting his existence as a person. No! It was this eternal Person, the Son of God, who now assumed this form and entered the life of man in the world."

- Lloyd-Jones 'Great Doctrines Series - Vol.1' p.253

Offices of Christ

In God's relationship with Israel he ordained three offices through which to deal with the people, the offices of prophet, priest, and king. Through the prophet he spoke to the people, directing and instructing; through the priest he mediated to the people forgiveness and reconciliation; through the king he reigned over the people. All these offices are seen in the person and work of Christ.

Christ our Prophet

As our prophet, Christ delivers us from the blindness of sin. The duty of the prophet was to reveal the will of God to the people. As prophet, Christ is God's full and final word to man, "but in these last days he has spoken to us by his Son," (Heb 1:2). He perfectly expressed all that was in the Father's heart, "For I did not speak on my own, but the Father who sent me commanded me to say all that I have spoken." (Jhn 12:49); "For I gave them the words you gave me and they accepted them. They knew with certainty that I came from you, and they believed that you sent me." (Jhn 17:8).

Christ our Priest

As our priest, Christ delivers us from the guilt of sin. What is a priest?

- One who represents others before God,
- One who offers sacrifices for the peoples sin.
- One who intercedes for the people.

All these things are clearly seen in the work that Jesus Christ came to fulfil.

1. He represents us as the only mediator between God and man, "For there is one God and one mediator between God and mankind, the man Christ Jesus," (1 Tim 2:5). He is also the mediator of the new covenant, "For this reason Christ is the mediator of a new covenant" (Heb 9:15).

2. He was not only the priest who brought a sacrifice to God, on the behalf of others, he himself was that sacrifice, "But he has appeared once for all at the culmination of the ages to do away with sin by the sacrifice of himself." (Heb 9:26).

3. On the basis of his sacrifice being sufficient to deal with sin and satisfy the holiness of God, Jesus intercedes for his people, "Christ Jesus who died--more than that, who was raised to life--is at the right hand of God and is also interceding for us" (Rom 8:34); "Therefore he is able to save completely those who come to God through him, because he always lives to intercede for them." (Heb 7:25).

✏ Assignment

What are the blessings that come to us as believers through knowing Christ as our High Priest?

Christ our King

As our king, Christ delivers us from the kingdom of darkness, the reign of sin and Satan, and brings us into his kingdom of righteousness. There are various expressions of the kingship of Christ,

1. Because he is equal with God the Father, he has always shared in the government of the universe, "Your throne, O God, will last for ever and ever; a sceptre of justice will be the sceptre of your kingdom." (Psa 45:6-7).

2. He is king over the true Israel, "Where is the one who has been born king of the Jews?" (Mat 2:2). "He will be great and will be called the Son of the Most High. The

Lord God will give him the throne of his father David, and he will reign over Jacob's descendants forever; his kingdom will never end." (Luk 1:32-33).

3. He is king of a spiritual kingdom that is ruling in the earth now, "Then the end will come, when he hands over the kingdom to God the Father after he has destroyed all dominion, authority and power. For he must reign until he has put all his enemies under his feet." (1 Cor 15:24-25)

4. In a future time he will be king of the new heaven and the new earth, "The kingdom of the world has become the kingdom of our Lord and of his Messiah, and he will reign for ever and ever." (Rev 11:15).

Conclusion

In all our attempts to understand the mystery of Christ we must not lean to his humanity and exclude his Deity. Nor must we lean to his divine nature to the exclusion of his real human nature. The Jesus who said, "for the Father is greater than I", also said, "I and the Father are one". Christ is equal to the Father as touching his Godhead and yet less than the Father as touching his manhood. The amazing thing, in all this, is that he did not grasp after his equality with God, "rather, he made himself nothing by taking the very nature of a servant," (Phi 2:6-7).

All this leads to the mystery of godliness, "Beyond all question, the mystery from which true godliness springs is great: He appeared in the flesh, was vindicated by the Spirit, was seen by angels, was preached among the nations, was believed on in the world, was taken up in glory." (1 Tim 3:16). The truth of Jesus the Son of God is too big for mere logic to comprehend. But, as with all the major truths of Scripture, we submit our intelligence to the revelation of God in His Word and believe with all our hearts.

✎ Assignment
Write an account of how you came to a personal faith in the Lord Jesus Christ.

Notes

God's Eternal Purpose

Study 4
The Doctrine of Man

📖 **Psalm 8**

The origin of man

The next big question after 'Who is God?' and 'Who is Jesus Christ?' is 'Who am I?' The answer we give to that question will deeply affect us, and our understanding of life. The psalmist asks the question, in the light of God's interest in him, "What is mankind that you are mindful of them?" (Psa 8:4). There are two obsessions in man's quest for knowledge:

1. Trying to understand ourselves - our origin, purpose and destiny (Where did I come from? Why am I here? Where am I going?).
2. Trying to understand the universe - its origin, purpose and destiny.

Man's quest to discover himself has been long and hard. His innate desire to understand his own position and role in the immensity of the universe has led him to clutch at straws. The theory that has dominated the minds of many in the western world is the theory of evolution. It teaches that the origin of the human species has evolved, over millions of years, from a globule of protoplasm, floating in the primeval deep, to the complex being he is today. As to our purpose, it is simply to produce the next generation, and as to our destiny it is the grave.

The Bible clearly teaches that man is a creature, i.e. he is made by a creator. He is part of the whole natural system that God created. The true, instinctive answer to the questions, 'Who am I?' 'Where do I come from?' is, "Know that the LORD is God. It is he who made us, and we are his; we are his people, the sheep of his pasture." (Psa 100:3).

As human beings we are a very special part of God's creation, because we were made in the image of God.

"So God created mankind in his own image, in the image of God he created them; male and female he created them." (Gen. 1:27,28). Since we were made in the likeness of God we are moral creatures, with an innate sense of what is right and wrong. It also means that we are more responsible to God than any of the other creatures. As human beings we must answer to God for our actions in life. The image of God in human nature is revealed in a very wonderful way through personality, spirituality, rationality, morality, authority, and creativity. All these things set us apart from, and above, the animal kingdom, and the rest of the created order in this world.

So what is our purpose in life?

"What is the chief end of man? Answer:- Man's chief end is to glorify God, and to enjoy him forever."

- The Westminster Shorter Catechism

✎ Assignment
In which ways has God set mankind apart from all other creatures?

The nature of man

Scripture uses various words to describe the make-up of human nature.

a) Hebrew *basar*; Greek *sarx* or *soma* - flesh or body.

b) Hebrew *nepes*; Greek *psyche* - soul.

c) Hebrew *ruach*; Greek *pneuma* - spirit.

Spirit

The deepest part of man is his spirit, which, although it is non-matter, is of real substance. It is out of this capacity of spirit that man relates to God and finds his highest function of worship, "God is spirit, and his worshippers must worship in the Spirit and in truth" (Jhn 4:24). With regard to the make-up of man, scripture uses the word 'spirit' in such a way that it overlaps the meaning of the word 'soul'. Indeed, it is very difficult for us to pull them apart. However, the word of God is said to divide between them, "For the word of God is alive and active. Sharper than any double-edged sword, it penetrates even to dividing soul and spirit ... it judges the thoughts and attitudes of the heart." (Heb 4:12). The human spirit is the source of person-hood, and self determination in man.

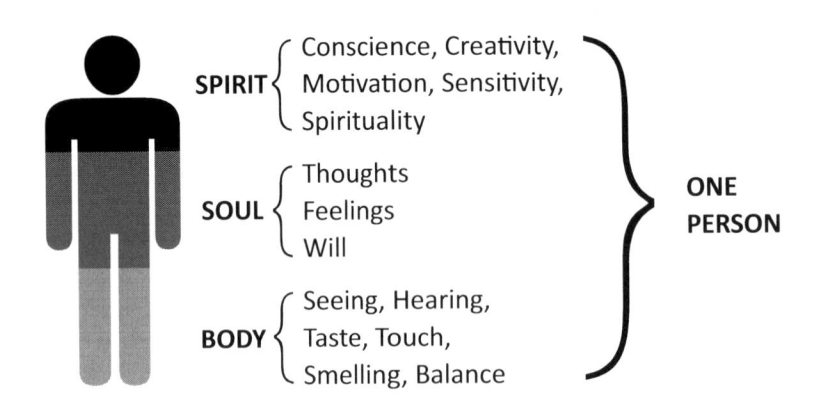

SPIRIT { Conscience, Creativity, Motivation, Sensitivity, Spirituality

SOUL { Thoughts, Feelings, Will

BODY { Seeing, Hearing, Taste, Touch, Smelling, Balance

} ONE PERSON

Soul

Man is more than physical body; he is a thinking, feeling, and willing creature. He has a personal awareness and a sense of identity that places him above all animals. Man is a living soul and, as such, he knows himself and relates to other people. It should be noted that the Bible sometimes uses the word soul to describe the whole person; we are souls, "and about three thousand (souls) were added to their number that day." (Act 2:41). The word describes our personal existence; it is the seat of the intellect and is marked by vital drives, and desires.

Body

Man has a physical body by which he relates to the material world around him. Through his five senses his body constantly receives information about his surroundings. The body is a marvel- lously structured organism. Its intricate cellular make-up is slowly being discovered by modern medical science. Long ago the psalmist saw it as a reason for worshipping God, "I praise you because I am fearfully and wonderfully made; your works are wonderful, I know that full well." (Psa 139:14).

Unity

It is often debated whether man is bi-partite or tri-partite. Is he composed of two parts, or three parts? In regard to the substance he is made of, he has two parts, material and non-material; body and spirit. In regard to the way he functions those two substances meet in soul; he is therefore tri-partite. In the Genesis account of creation it says, "Then the LORD God formed a man from the dust of the ground (body) and breathed into his nostrils the breath of life (spirit), and the man became a living being (soul)." (Gen 2:7). Paul uses this trilogy of words to refer to the make-up of human nature, "May your whole spirit, soul and body be kept blameless at the coming of our Lord Jesus Christ." (1 The 5:23). We should, however, be careful not to try and divide human nature up into separate parts. We are not separate elements that can be taken apart for analysis; we are made as whole persons without division.

Man in innocence

"This only have I found: God created mankind upright, but they have gone in search of many schemes." (Ecc 7:29). We were made in the moral image of God, with original righteousness, "So God created mankind in his own image" (Gen 1:27). Adam had a clear knowledge of what was right, with an inbuilt inclination that way. He was not perfected in holiness, but had a natural love for holiness.

- **He was made for fellowship with God**, "Then the man and his wife heard the sound of the LORD God as he was walking in the garden in the cool of the day," (Gen 3:8-9).

- **He was made with the possibility of immortality**, "for when you eat from it you will certainly die." (Gen 2:17). God was saying that death would only come as a result of sin.

- **He was clothed with a God given glory**, "You have made them a little lower than the angels and crowned them with glory and honour." (Psa 8:5).

- **He was made well pleasing to God**, "God saw all that he had made, and it was very good." (Gen 1:31).

Man in the fall

The effects of the fall of Adam and Eve into sin extend to all parts of creation. The whole of nature is out of order, "We know that the whole creation has been groaning as in the pains of childbirth right up to the present time." (Rom 8:22). Sin has affected us as human beings in a particular way because it has broken our relationship with God and brought us into a relationship with Satan. Jesus exposed this fact when he said to the Pharisees, "You belong to your father, the devil, and you want to carry out your father's desires" (Jhn 8:44). Adam gave away his rights of rulership over the world and put himself in bondage to Satan. So, man's problem is not just that he sins by breaking the law. That is a symptom of the problem. The problem is that sin is deeply rooted in the will of man, it is an active rebellion against God that has broken his relationship with God, "As at Adam, they have broken the covenant; they were unfaithful to me there." (Hos 6:7).

- **Sin brought decay and death to our physical bodies**, "By the sweat of your brow you will eat your food until you return to the ground, since from it you were taken; for dust you are and to dust you will return." (Gen 3:19).

- **Sin brought spiritual separation between us and God**, " So the LORD God banished him from the Garden of Eden to work the ground from which he had been taken." (Gen 3:23-24).

- **Sin damaged our emotions**, "Therefore God gave them over in the sinful desires of their hearts" (Rom 1:24).

- **Sin brought inability to work righteousness**, "As it is written: There is no one righteous, not even one; there is no one who understands; there is no one who seeks God." (Rom 3:10-11).

The image of God is still in us but it is distorted through our fallenness, and consequently every human being is imperfect. We are still capable of doing acts of human goodness. However, because of the effects of sin upon our nature we can never bring our acts as righteous before God, "All of us have become like one who is unclean, and all our righteous acts are like filthy rags;" (Isa 64:6).

> *The sin of Adam has affected all of us, because he stood as the head of the human race.*

The problem is not just that we do sinful things, but that in our very constitution we are fallen, "Surely I was sinful at birth, sinful from the time my mother conceived me." (Psa 51:5). All the calamities of life, its injustice, misery, pain etc., can all be traced back to that tragic happening in the Garden of Eden.

Adam capitulated to God's enemy and lost his righteousness, his freedom, his immortality, his ruler-ship and his friendship with God. In his fall Adam surrendered his lordship rites over this world. He gave to the devil the very authority that God had given him. The sin of Adam has affected all of us, because he stood as the head of the human race. As a result the whole world has come under condemnation, "Therefore, just as sin entered the world through one man, and death through sin, and in this way death came to all people, because all sinned--" (Rom 5:12, see also v19 - not 'have sinned', but 'all sinned' in the one act of Adam). Outside of the grace of God we were spiritually dead, "As for you, you were dead in your transgressions and sins," (Eph 2:1). We were guilty before God, "Now we know that whatever the law says, it says to those who are under the law, so that every mouth may be silenced and the whole world held accountable to God." (Rom 3:19). We were enslaved to the devil, "and escape from the trap of the devil, who has taken them captive to do his will." (2 Tim 2:26).

"There is therefore, no 'sinful human nature'. Such an understanding leads right into the jaws of Hellenism where Christian truth is devoured. Rather than speaking of the NIV's 'sinful nature', we must learn to speak of the 'fallen condition' of man. He is born in Adam, and in that state he can neither please God nor know him. ... Sin is not found, therefore, within a distorted human nature. It is the result of Satan enslaving the will of man."

- Holland 'Romans: The Divine Marriage' p.224

✎ Assignment
What are some of the effects of sin on mankind and our environment?

Man in grace

We were unclean and rebellious toward God, and the image of God in us was spoiled. However, God still looked on us with mercy and love. He never gave up on his original plan to have his image reflected in mankind through both male and female.

We were rebels, but we were loved rebels.

However, God could only act in salvation in accord with his own holy nature. Therefore, a way had to be made for God's holiness to be satisfied and for sinners to be justified. God did that through the death of his Son, "You see, at just the right time, when we were still powerless, Christ died for the ungodly." (Rom 5:6). God has made a way for men and women to be reconciled to himself, "Once you were alienated from God and were enemies in your minds because of your evil behaviour. But now he has reconciled you by Christ's physical body through death" (Col 1:21-22).

All this was purchased for us by the atoning sacrifice of Christ and is appropriated through a commitment of faith, "God presented Christ as a sacrifice of atonement, through the shedding of his blood--to be received by faith." (Rom 3:25). God quickens the sinner from his spiritual death to newness of life. This is spoken of by Jesus in terms of a new birth, "Very truly I tell you, no one can see the kingdom of God unless they are born again." (Jhn 3:3). It is spoken of by Paul as a new creation, "Therefore, if anyone is in Christ, the new creation has come: The old has gone, the new is here!" (2 Cor 5:17). Whatever Adam lost for mankind in his fall has been more than restored for us through the Lord Jesus Christ. Adam only just began to discover his status as a son of God and was not perfected in holiness. Christ completed every test and has revealed the heights of that sonship for us.

Man in death

There is a note of finality in the scripture, "Just as people are destined to die once, and after that to face judgement," (Heb 9:27). Paul shows how the sin of Adam led to death coming upon all mankind, "Therefore, just as sin entered the world through one man, and death through sin, and in this way death came to all people, because all sinned" (Rom 5:12). Apart from two notable exceptions, Enoch and Elijah, death has been the common experience of all. Both believers and unbelievers end this life in the same way.

Death in medical terms is merely the ceasing of the function of vital organs of the body and a cessation of the electro impulses of the brain. But in Bible terms it is the separation of the spirit from the body, "and the dust returns to the ground it came from, and the spirit returns to God who gave it." (Ecc 12:7). We see this in the death of Christ, "With that, he bowed his head and gave up his spirit." (Jhn 19:30).

Though death is the common lot of all men, there is a marked difference in what happens to the righteous and what happens to the unrighteous at death.

1a. **God takes no pleasure in the death of the wicked**, "As surely as I live, declares the Sovereign LORD, I take no pleasure in the death of the wicked, but rather that they turn from their ways and live" (Eze 33:11).

1b. **The death of saints is precious to God**, "Precious in the sight of the LORD is the death of his faithful servants" (Psa 116:15).

2a. **The wicked are blown away at death**, "Not so the wicked! They are like chaff that the wind blows away." (Psa 1:4).

2b. **The righteous fall asleep in Christ**, "so we believe that God will bring with Jesus those who have fallen asleep in him." (1 The 4:14).

3a. **The wicked are swallowed up in wrath**, "The LORD will swallow them up in his wrath, and his fire will consume them." (Psa 21:9).

3b. **The righteous gain in death**, "I am torn between the two: I desire to depart and be with Christ, which is better by far;" (Phi 1:23).

✎ Assignment
What happens to the righteous immediately after death? *(see Phi 1:23, 2 Cor 5:6)*

Man in final judgement

The wicked at death are brought to a waiting place in which there is anguish of soul, "In Hades, where he was in torment, he looked up and saw Abraham far away, with Lazarus by his side." (Luk 16:23). At the end of time all mankind will be brought to the final judgement, "but only a fearful expectation of judgement and of raging fire that will consume the enemies of God." (Heb 10:27). The wicked will be raised in bodies of death and appear before the "Great White Throne of God", (Rev 20:12). They will receive the just dues for their deeds, for God is a righteous judge.

All that is in opposition to God and his Christ will be cast into the lake of fire and brimstone, "Anyone whose name was not found written in the book of life was thrown into the lake of fire." (Rev 20:14-15). This Judgement will seal their fate for ever, "And the smoke of their torment will rise for ever and ever." (Rev 14:11).

Man in future glory

The state of the redeemed dead is completely the opposite to that of the lost. They are described as "the spirits of the righteous made perfect," (Heb 12:23). They leave these mortal bodies and go into the presence of Christ, "We are confident, I say, and would prefer to be away from the body and at home with the Lord." (2 Cor 5:8). They will return with Christ, be given new glorified bodies, and, along with living saints, will be with Christ forever, "For the Lord himself will come down from heaven, with a loud command, with the voice of the archangel and with the trumpet call of God, and the dead in Christ will rise first. After that, we who are still alive and are left will be caught up together with them in the clouds to meet the Lord in the air. And so we will be with the Lord forever." (1 The 4:13-17). Every effect of sin will be done away with, "No longer will there be any curse. The throne of God and of the Lamb will be in the city, and his servants will serve him." (Rev 22:3).

They will be linked with Christ in a great eternal purpose and share his ruler-ship of the new creation. "They will see his face, and his name will be on their foreheads ... And they shall reign for ever and ever." (Rev 22:4-5).

Notes

God's Eternal Purpose

Study 5

The Doctrine of Salvation

📖 **Ephesians 2:1-13**

Introduction

"If I understand the New Testament aright, there is no place where we should be more careful to go with our minds fully operating as to the cross on Calvary's hill. And I will tell you why: it is because this is the central thing; there is no truth concerning which the adversary and the enemy of our souls is so anxious to muddle and confuse us as this particular truth."

- Lloyd-Jones 'Great Doctrines' p.308

The whole theme of salvation in the Scripture is a very great one. The message of salvation, through the atoning death of Christ, makes Christianity stand out from all other religions. The fact that sinners, deserving the wrath of God, can be brought back into a loving relationship with him is amazing. There are several important words used in scripture to describe what God has done for us, in bringing us back into a right relationship with himself. A study of them will show us how extensive and complete our salvation is. All these themes take us back into the Old Testament where God gave insights into the way of salvation through 'types and shadows'. The need of salvation comes because of the holiness of God and because of our fallen state. Sin is direct rebellion against God from man's side and a violation of holiness from God's side.

In the whole theme of salvation the cross stands at the centre of all that God does in Christ. It was not just a tragic accident of politics gone wrong. The cross is not about the untimely death of a martyr giving himself for a cause. The cross is the very reason why Christ came into the world, and it is the very basis of our salvation. Christ's death is not just an expression of the love of God - though it is that. Nor is Jesus merely setting an example for us in how to bear suffering. The cross is about God's absolute justice and holiness being satisfied. It enabled him to forgive sinners and bring them back into a position of honour with himself. It involved the overthrow of Satan's power and lordship over the world. It involved the restoration of redeemed mankind back to a position of sonship-authority. Through the cross the eternal purpose of God for his creation was restored.

✎ Assignment
Show from Scripture the importance of the cross of Christ in God's plan of Salvation.
(see 1 Cor 1:18, 1 Cor 2:2 and Gal 6:14)

Salvation

The meaning of the Greek word for salvation, 'soteria' is to rescue from danger and harm by bringing to a place of safety. Its use, with regard to God's people, involves the whole system of God's grace. It rescues us from the penalty of sin and the tyranny of Satan, and brings us into a place of safety and well being in Christ.

- **It is found only in the name and person of Christ**, "Salvation is found in no one else, for there is no other name under heaven given to mankind by which we must be saved" (Act 4:12).

- **It is revealed to us in the scripture**, "and how from infancy you have known the Holy Scriptures, which are able to make you wise for salvation through faith in Christ Jesus." (2 Tim 3:15).

- **It is brought to us through repentance**, "Godly sorrow brings repentance that leads to salvation and leaves no regret, but worldly sorrow brings death." (2 Cor 7:10).

- **It is received by submissive faith in Christ's Lordship**, "If you declare with your mouth, 'Jesus is Lord,' and believe in your heart that God raised him from the dead, you will be saved. For it is with your heart that you believe and are justified, and it is with your mouth that you profess your faith and are saved." (Rom 10:9-10).

- **It is something that begins now**, "I tell you, now is the time of God's favour, now is the day of salvation." (2 Cor 6:2).

- **It is progressively worked out in our lives**, "--continue to work out your salvation with fear and trembling," (Phi 2:12).

- **It will be fully realised at Christ's coming**, "and he will appear a second time, not to bear sin, but to bring salvation to those who are waiting for him." (Heb 9:28).

Atonement and Propitiation

The atonement is the work that Christ accomplished by his sacrificial death, in order to bring about our salvation. In the Old Testament the Hebrew word 'kaphar' is repeatedly used, which basically means to cover over. But the implication is that it is the covering of a wrong by the use of a sacrifice that makes amends. It is linked, in the New Testament with the word 'propitiation' which is sometimes translated 'atonement'.

Atonement has reference to sin, "Sacrifice a bull each day as a sin offering to make atonement." (Exo 29:36). It is always obtained through the shedding of blood, "For the life of a creature is in the blood, and I have given it to you to make atonement for yourselves on the altar; it is the blood that makes atonement for one's life." (Lev 17:11). This is stated again in Hebrews, "In fact, the law requires that nearly everything be cleansed with blood, and without the shedding of blood there is no forgiveness." (Heb 9:22).

It was the love and justice of God that led to Christ coming to earth and dying for our sins. The verse "For God so loved the world that he gave his one and only Son," (Jhn 3:16) speaks of the love of God that led to him sending Christ. But a holy God would be unjust to forgive sinners without a penalty being

> *Christ took the penalty for our sins upon himself, and became the means of satisfying the holiness and justice of God.*

paid. Thus, Christ took the penalty for our sins upon himself and became the means of satisfying the holiness and justice of God, "He is the atoning sacrifice for our sins, and not only for ours but also for the sins of the whole world." (1 Jhn 2:2). John further states, "This is love: not that we loved God, but that he loved us and sent his Son as an atoning sacrifice for our sins." (1 Jhn 4:10).

Christ bore the wrath of God against sin, and so God is just when he allows the believing sinner to go free, "God presented Christ as a sacrifice of atonement, through the shedding of his blood ... he did it to demonstrate his righteousness at the present time, so as to be just and the one who justifies those who have faith in Jesus." (Rm.3:25,26). The Lord Jesus Christ suffered the penalty of the broken law vicariously (on behalf of others) as the substitute for sinners. He became the fulfilment of all the OT sacrifices which were offered as a substitute for the offerer, "The blood of goats and bulls and the ashes of a heifer sprinkled on those who are ceremonially unclean sanctify them so that they are outwardly clean. How much more, then, will the blood of Christ, who through the eternal Spirit offered himself unblemished to God, cleanse our consciences from acts that lead to death, so that we may serve the living God!" (Heb 9:13-14, see also 2 Cor 5:21).

✏ Assignment
What is the significance of the shedding of blood in the work of atonement?

Redemption

The word 'Redemption' often brings the picture of slavery and a ransom price being paid. Unbelievers are in a system of bondage to sin and Satan, "We know that we are children of God, and that the whole world is under the control of the evil one." (1 Jhn 5:19). Christ said of himself, "For even the Son of Man did not come to be served, but to serve, and to give his life as a ransom for many" (Mar 10:45). Christ paid a price for us in order that we might be made children of God, "to redeem those under the law, that we might receive adoption to sonship." (Gal 4:5). The whole picture of Redemption takes us back to the action of God in 'Redeeming' his people from Egypt. This intervention of God became the basis of his claim to Israel's allegiance. Through the Passover sacrifice each family was saved from the wrath of God and the first-born kept in safety. From that point on every first-born belonged to God and constantly reminded his people that they had been delivered by him. Christ, as God's first-born, was sacrificed and became our Passover lamb, "Get rid of the old yeast, so that you may be a new unleavened batch--as you really are. For Christ, our Passover lamb, has been sacrificed." (1 Cor 5:7).

- **We were redeemed from the curse of the law**, "Christ redeemed us from the curse of the law by becoming a curse for us" (Gal 3:13).

- **We were redeemed from wicked works**, "who gave himself for us to redeem us from all wickedness and to purify for himself a people that are his very own, eager to do what is good." (Tit 2:14).

- **The purchase price was the blood of Christ**, "For you know that it was not with perishable things such as silver or gold that you were redeemed ... but with the precious blood of Christ, a lamb without blemish or defect." (1 Pet 1:18-19).

- **The purchase price was for a bride**, "Husbands, love your wives, just as Christ loved the church and gave himself up for her" (Eph 5:25, see also 1 Cor 6:20).

Reconciliation

We were separated from God because of sin, and our hearts were at enmity against him. So sin is firstly the breaking of a covenant relationship, and then the breaking of the law. To overcome this separation we needed someone to bring about a reconciliation so that we could have fellowship with a holy God. Paul tells us "For if, while we were God's enemies, we were reconciled to him through the death of his Son, how much more, having been reconciled, shall we be saved through his life!" (Rom 5:10). God's love was so great that he took the initiative in reconciling us back to himself, "All this is from God, who reconciled us to himself through Christ" (2 Cor 5:18).

All these things were brought about by the sacrificial death of Christ. We do not contribute any good thing towards our salvation. We enter this salvation through the commitment of faith, and by the amazing grace of God, "For it is by grace you have been saved, through faith--and this is not from yourselves, it is the gift of God-- not by works, so that no one can boast." (Eph 2:8-9).

Calling

The word 'calling' epitomises God taking a personal interest in the life of the person who comes to Christ through the Gospel. It carries the same picture as the account of God seeking after Adam in the garden of Eden, "But the LORD God called to the man, 'Where are you'?" (Gen 3:9). Paul set out a series of blessings that are directed towards those who know salvation in the Lord Jesus Christ, "And those he predestined, he also called; those he called, he also justified; those he justified, he also glorified." (Rom 8:30).

We are called through the gospel:

- **From darkness to light**, "But you are a chosen people, a royal priesthood, a holy nation, God's special possession, that you may declare the praises of him who called you out of darkness into his wonderful light." (1 Pet 2:9).

- **Into fellowship with God's Son**, "God is faithful, who has called you into fellowship with his Son, Jesus Christ our Lord." (1 Cor 1:9).

- **Into God's kingdom and glory**, "encouraging, comforting and urging you to live lives worthy of God, who calls you into his kingdom and glory." (1 The 2:11-12).

- **To be God's holy people**, "To the church of God in Corinth, to those sanctified in Christ Jesus and called to be his holy people," (1 Cor 1:2).

Adoption

The salvation brought about by the death and resurrection of Jesus the Christ is not just about sinners receiving the forgiveness of sins. In submitting to Christ's Lord-ship those sinners are brought into a new relationship with God. The outcome of that relationship is that we are given the high status as sons of God. We lost that status in Adam, who was called a son of God, when God created him, (Luk 3:38). Our sonship is restored through the Last Adam. Christ was called the Son of God, not only as the eternal, 'only begotten son', but also as Messiah. Through Redemption we are linked with that Messiah-sonship, "In bringing many sons and daughters to glory, it was fitting that God ... should make the pioneer of their salvation perfect through what he suffered." (Heb 2:10).

- **We are made sons of God by the will of God**, "Yet to all who did receive him, to those who believed in his name, he gave the right to become children of God-- children born not of natural descent, nor of human decision or a husband's will, but born of God." (Jhn 1:12-13).

- **We are made sons by adoption into God's family**, "to redeem those under the law, that we might receive adoption to sonship." (Gal 4:5).

- **As sons we bare the image of God**, "and have put on the new self (new man), which is being renewed in knowledge in the image of its Creator." (Col 3:10).

- **As sons we are greatly loved of God**, "See what great love the Father has lavished on us, that we should be called children of God! And that is what we are!" (1 Jhn 3:1).

- **As sons we are given assurance by the Spirit**, "The Spirit you received does not make you slaves, so that you live in fear again; rather, the Spirit you received brought about your adoption to sonship. And by him we cry, 'Abba, Father'." (Rom 8:15).

Justification

Justification is a comprehensive term that is used in several ways in Scripture, to speak of God's action towards those who put their trust in him. We look at it briefly within two settings. The one in which God freely forgives the sinner, and the other in which God brings believers into covenant.

To free from guilt

The main meaning of 'justification' is 'to acquit from fault', or 'declare righteous'. It is a legal term that was used in the law courts to express the judge's verdict in acquitting the accused person. So, in a Christian context, justification is an act of God in which he freely pardons our sins and accepts us as righteous. This is done on the basis of the righteousness of Christ being imputed to us. It was in this context that Paul used the example of David, as someone who had sinned against God and yet found forgiveness and acquittal in God's sight, "David says the same thing when he speaks of the blessedness of the one to whom God credits righteousness apart from works: 'Blessed are those whose transgressions are forgiven, whose sins are covered. Blessed is the one whose sin the Lord will never count against them'" (Rom 4:5-8).

To bring into covenant

Another way in which the word 'Justification' is used in Scripture is brought out in God's dealings with Abraham. Abraham is said to have been justified before God when he believed that God would give him a son by Sarah, "Abram believed the LORD, and he credited it to him as righteousness." (Gen 15:6). In this incident God was declaring Abraham to be righteous (right with God) and entering into a covenant with him (Gen 15:7-21). It is noticeable in this case that God is not dealing with any sinful behaviour of Abraham, but, commending him for having believed the word that God spoke to him.

The means of justification – faith and repentance

How, then, is the sinner to be justified before God? The answer of scripture is 'by faith', "For we maintain that a person is **justified by faith** apart from the works of the law." (Rom 3:28). It is not that faith earns or merits our being justified, but it is the means by which it is received. Thus, God accounts those righteous who believe on his Son, "This righteousness is given **through faith** in Jesus Christ to all who believe." (Rom 3:22). Faith is not some nominal belief in historic facts, but a whole hearted commitment to Jesus Christ as Lord, and a deep trust in what he has done for us by his death. Although faith is the product of the human heart, "For it is with your heart that you believe and are justified," (Rom 10:10), it is by the grace of God that we are drawn to it, "When he (*Apollus*) arrived, he was a great help to those who **by grace** had believed." (Act 18:27). Similarly, we are called to repent of our sinful ways. Repentance is not just feeling sorry for our sin, but a change of heart towards God that leads to a change of behaviour. It is we who have to repent. God does not repent for us. However, we need his kindness to lead us to it, "not realising that God's kindness is intended to lead you to repentance?" (Rom 2:4).

Justification changes our standing before God. He accepts us as righteous. Therefore, our position in being justified does not vary according to our feelings or experience. It remains constant; we cannot be more or less justified.

✎ Assignment
Show the importance of the doctrine of Justification.

Sanctification

The meaning of the word 'sanctification', and its counterpart 'holiness', is 'separated for sacred use', and implies purity. The importance of the believer being sanctified is expressed in the statement, "without holiness no one will see the Lord." (Heb 12:14). It is expressly stated as the will of God for all believers, "It is God's will that you should be sanctified" (1 The 4:3). Sanctification is really to do with the renewing of the image of God in us, which is the ultimate goal of God's purpose for us, "For those God foreknew he also predestined to be conformed to the image of his Son," (Rom 8:29).

What is involved in sanctification?

It can be viewed from different standpoints in the scripture.

1. Jeremiah was sanctified before he was born, "Before I formed you in the womb I knew you, before you were born I set you apart (*sanctified*);" (Jer 1:5). This cannot mean that Jeremiah was morally changed before he was born. It is speaking of God's action in choosing Jeremiah, as a prophet.

2. All believers are positionally sanctified, in the sense that we are separated unto God, "And so Jesus also suffered outside the city gate to make the people holy through his own blood." (Heb 13:12). Believers were not morally changed when Christ suffered and died, but they were purchased and set apart for God.

3. Sanctification has to do with a moral transformation or renewal of our whole character, in which we take an active part, "Just as you used to offer yourselves as slaves to impurity ... so now offer yourselves as slaves to righteousness leading to holiness." (Rom 6:19).

Holiness involves both a separating from that which is unclean, and a separating unto that which is holy. The fall of Adam has affected the whole make-up of human nature, body, soul, and spirit, and consequently the image of God in mankind is spoiled. Sanctification has to do with restoring us back into the image of God, "and have put on the new self (new man), which is being renewed in knowledge in the image of its Creator." (Col 3:10).

The means of sanctification

1. Sanctification is purchased for us through the sacrifice of Christ, (Heb 13:12). In this respect Christ has become "for us wisdom from God--that is, our righteousness, holiness and redemption." (1 Cor 1:30). By his death he purchased us and separated us to God. He represents us as perfect before the Father, and he is the very pattern of our sanctification, "But now he has reconciled you by Christ's physical body through death to present you holy in his sight, without blemish and free from accusation--" (Col 1:22, see also Eph 5:25-27).

2. The Holy Spirit is seen as the one chiefly used in changing our character,"so that the Gentiles might become an offering acceptable to God, sanctified by the Holy Spirit." (Rom 15:16). Peter also deals with this truth, "who have been chosen according to the foreknowledge of God the Father, through the sanctifying work of the Spirit, to be obedient to Jesus Christ ..." (1 Pet 1:2).

3. The moral change in the believer focuses on a renewing of the mind, "You were taught, with regard to your former way of life, to put off your old self (man), which is being corrupted by its deceitful desires; to be made new in the attitude of your minds;" (Eph 4:22-23). The Holy Spirit enlightens the mind and diffuses a power into the personality enabling us to, walk "in the light, as he is in the light," (1 Jhn 1:7).

> *The moral change in a believer focuses on a renewing of the mind.*

4. This work of the Spirit is mainly accomplished through the word of God being received into the life. Jesus prayed for this, "Sanctify them by the truth; your word is

truth." (Jhn 17:17). Paul taught this truth, "to make her holy, cleansing her by the washing with water through the word," (Eph 5:26). The Holy Spirit in applying the word of God to the mind changes attitudes and actions and the word of Christ is fulfilled, "Then you will know the truth, and the truth will set you free." (Jhn 8:32).

5. The believer is also active in this work of renewal. We are told " let us purify ourselves from everything that contaminates body and spirit, perfecting holiness out of reverence for God." (2 Cor 7:1). We are exhorted, "Put to death, therefore, whatever belongs to your earthly nature: sexual immorality, impurity, lust, evil desires and greed, which is idolatry." (Col 3:5).

Thus, sanctification is through faith and works. Because it is all purchased by the sacrifice of Christ it must be entered through faith. However, it requires our co-operation in obedience to God's word, and so it is by works as well. To be remade in the image of God is to be our main goal in life.

Assignment
What should believers do to grow in a life of holiness?

The fullness of sanctification

The whole work of sanctification can be both advanced and retarded in the life of the believer. A work wrought on the heart can be undone by disobedience, "For the flesh desires what is contrary to the Spirit, and the Spirit what is contrary to the flesh. They are in conflict with each other, so that you are not to do whatever you want." (Gal 5:17). On the other hand the sanctifying work of the Spirit can be diffused through the believer to such an extent that we can be preserved blameless, "May God himself, the God of peace, sanctify you through and through. May your whole spirit, soul and body be kept blameless at the coming of our Lord Jesus Christ." (1 The 5:23). This does not bring us to a state of sinlessness, as human nature is defective in all its faculties, "If we claim to be without sin, we deceive ourselves and the truth is not in us." (1 Jhn 1:8). Our present experience of sanctification is a foretaste of what we will be in the 'age to come'. In the future age there will be no sinful behaviour to annoy or temptation to distract. However, through the sanctifying power of the Holy Spirit the believer can triumph over the 'spirit of this age' "and the evil one cannot harm them." (1 Jhn 5:18). We must wait until the coming of Christ for our perfect state, "and what we will be has not yet been made known. But we know that when Christ appears, we shall be like him, for we shall see him as he is." (1 Jhn 3:2).

Thus, sanctification should not be thought of as a fixed point, to be reached without further growth or change. It is rather, a principle that is suffused through the whole person, making clean the motives of the heart, and in which we are, "being transformed into his image with ever-increasing glory, which comes from the Lord, who is the Spirit." (2 Cor 3:18).

Notes

God's Eternal Purpose

Study 6
The Doctrine of the Spirit

📖 **John 16:5-15**

Introduction

The very name 'Holy Spirit' conveys a sense of mystery to us. How can we understand Divine Spirit? However, the Holy Spirit has come to take the mysteries of God and reveal them to us. He has come into the world to make the things of God, and salvation, real in our lives. The Holy Spirit is the divine person who brings about God's eternal purpose in the world.

He is the experienced presence of God.

"The Holy Scriptures declare him (Holy Spirit) to be the revealer of all truth, the active agent in all works of redemption, and from first to last the instrument of Grace in the experience of salvation. In him, and through him, and by him, is the power that saves. Illumination and Conviction, Repentance, and Regeneration, Assurance and Sanctification, are all the work of God the eternal Spirit ... He directs, energises, and controls. From first to last this dispensation is the dispensation of the Spirit."

— Chadwick 'The Way to Pentecost' p.9

The use of 'spirit' in Scripture

The name that the scripture gives to the third person of Trinity is, 'Spirit' or 'Holy Spirit'. The word 'spirit', from the Hebrew *ruach*, and Greek *pneuma*, means wind, breath, or spirit. The use of these words in scripture is not limited to the Spirit of God, but is used in various contexts.

- **Strong wind** – "The wind blows wherever it pleases." (Jhn 3:8); "and he sent a wind (ruach) over the earth, and the waters receded." (Gen 8:1). Both verses depict a strong wind.

- **Gentle wind** – "Then the man and his wife heard the sound of the LORD God as he

God's Eternal Purpose: An introduction to Christian doctrine

was walking in the garden in the cool (*ruach*) of the day," (Gen3:8). Here a soft, gentle movement of air is implied.

- **Vanity** – "The prophets are but wind (*ruach*) and the word is not in them;" (Jer 5:13). This is metaphorically used to signify instability and emptiness.
- **Points of the compass** – "and they will gather his elect from the four winds, from one end of the heavens to the other." (Mat 24:31).
- **Breath** – "Everything on dry land that had the breath (*ruach*) of life in its nostrils died." (Gen 7:22).
- **Affection of the soul** – "and when he saw the carts Joseph had sent to carry him back, the spirit of their father Jacob revived." (Gen 45:27).
- **Angels** – "He makes winds (*ruach*) his messengers, flames of fire his servants." (Psa 104:4). These are the unfallen, obedient angels.
- **Evil Spirits** – "I will go out and be a deceiving spirit in the mouths of all his prophets," (1 Kgs 22:22). "Jesus cured many who had diseases, sicknesses and evil spirits," (Luk 7:21).

Although there is such a variety of use for the word 'spirit' in scripture, there is little difficulty in seeing what its meaning is within context.

The Holy Spirit

There is a further use of the word 'spirit' in the Bible which reveals to us the very Spirit of God as separate and distinct from all other spirits. There are many references to the Holy Spirit in scripture which:

1. Refer to the person of the Holy Spirit.
2. Refer to the attributes and character of the Holy Spirit.
3. Refer to the relationship of the Holy Spirit to the Father and the Son.
4. Refer to the works of the Holy Spirit.

The personality of the Spirit

Some have denied that the Holy Spirit is a person. They regard him as a mere emanation of power from God. However, the Scripture clearly speaks of the Spirit as a distinct, divine perso. "The Spirit himself testifies with our spirit that we are God's children" (Rom 8:6). "The Spirit of the LORD will rest on him" (Isa 11:2). "How much more will your heavenly Father give the Holy Spirit to those who ask him!" (Luk 11:13).

> *The Scripture clearly speaks of the Holy Spirit as a distinct, divine person.*

The personal pronouns

In the great discourse that Jesus gave on the Holy Spirit, in John chapters 15 and 16, the Lord constantly used the personal pronouns 'he' and 'him' to describe the Spirit, (see Jhn 15:26, Jhn 16:7-8,13-15). The use of these pronouns is all the more remarkable as we consider that the Greek noun *pneuma* is neuter and the pronoun that refers to a neuter noun should itself be neuter. But scripture sets aside the point of grammar for the sake of preserving truth.

Personal properties of the Spirit

Personality must have certain properties by which it can be known and expressed. The basic properties of personality are intelligence, self awareness, and power of will. The scripture pieces together a picture of the Holy Spirit that is so complete it leaves us in no doubt that he is a real person,

- **The Holy Spirit reveals things to believers**, "What no eye has seen, what no ear has heard, and what no human mind has conceived" - the things God has prepared for those who love him - these are the things God has revealed to us by his Spirit. The Spirit searches all things, even the deep things of God. For who knows a person's thoughts except their own spirit within them? In the same way no one knows the thoughts of God except the Spirit of God." (1 Cor 2:9-16).

- **The Holy Spirit exercises will**, "All these are the work of one and the same Spirit, and he distributes them to each one, just as he determines." (1 Cor 12:11).

- **The Holy Spirit has personal power**, "The Spirit of God has made me; the breath of the Almighty gives me life." (Job 33:4). Jesus promised his followers, "But you will receive power when the Holy Spirit comes on you;" (Act 1:8).

Personal senses of the Spirit

Perhaps it is difficult for us to grasp the sensitivity of the Spirit. We cannot see any physical feature that would reveal hurt or pain. However, the scripture reveals this aspect of the personality of the Spirit of God.

- **The Holy Spirit can be lied to**, "Ananias, how is it that Satan has so filled your heart that you have lied to the Holy Spirit?" (Act 5:3).

- **The Holy Spirit can be tempted (tested)**, "How could you conspire to test the Spirit of the Lord?" (Act 5:9).

- **The Holy Spirit can be grieved**, "And do not grieve the Holy Spirit of God, with whom you were sealed for the day of redemption." (Eph 4:30).

- **The Holy Spirit can be sinned against**, "but whoever blasphemes against the Holy Spirit will never be forgiven;" (Mar 3:29).

- **The Holy Spirit can be resisted**, "You are just like your ancestors: You always resist the Holy Spirit!" (Act 7:51).

✎ Assignment
How can we develop an intimate relationship with the Holy Spirit?

The attributes of the Spirit

The very character and attributes of God shine out of the Bible's presentation of the Holy Spirit. Numerous sections of

the scripture, when pieced together, make up a glorious picture of this divine person.

- **He is the Spirit of holiness**, "and who through the Spirit of holiness was appointed the Son of God in power by his resurrection" (Rom 1:4).
- **He is the Spirit of truth**, "But when he, the Spirit of truth, comes, he will guide you into all the truth." (Jhn 16:13).
- **He is the Spirit of life**, "because through Christ Jesus the law of the Spirit who gives life has set you free from the law of sin and death." (Rom 8:2).
- **He is the Spirit of wisdom**, "The Spirit of the LORD shall rest upon him, the Spirit of wisdom and understanding"(Isa 11:2).
- **He is the Spirit of counsel and might** (Isa 11:2).
- **He is the Spirit of knowledge, and the fear of the LORD** (Isa 11:2).
- **He is the Spirit of grace**, "How much more severely do you think someone deserves to be punished ... and who has insulted the Spirit of grace?" (Heb 10:29).
- **He is the Spirit of glory**, "for the Spirit of glory and of God rests on you." (1 Pet 4:14).

The relationship of the Spirit to Father and Son

The doctrine of Trinity in scripture is a very glorious one. The intimate relationship between the three persons in Godhead has always been a source of wonder, and a reason for worship, in the heart of the believer. There are scriptures that show something of the relationship of the Holy Spirit to God the Father and to God the Son. Jesus tells us that the Spirit proceeds from the Father and is sent by the Son, "When the Advocate comes, whom I will send to you from the Father--the Spirit of truth who goes out from the Father--he will testify about me." (Jhn 15:26).

- **He is called the Spirit of Yahweh**, "The Spirit of the Sovereign LORD is on me," (Isa 61:1).
- **He is called the Spirit of the living God**, "You show that you are a letter from Christ ... written not with ink but with the Spirit of the living God," (2 Cor 3:3).
- **He is called the Spirit of Christ**, "And if anyone does not have the Spirit of Christ, they do not belong to Christ." (Rom 8:9).
- **He is called the Spirit of his Son**, "Because you are his sons, God sent the Spirit of his Son into our hearts," (Gal 4:6).
- **He is called the Spirit of Jesus Christ**, "for I know that through your prayers and God's provision of the Spirit of Jesus Christ what has happened to me will turn out for my deliverance." (Phi 1:19).
- **He is called the Spirit of your Father**, "for it will not be you speaking, but the Spirit of your Father speaking through you." (Mat 10:20).

The work of the Spirit in the world

The works that are attributed to the Holy Spirit are works that only God can do. Only God can produce something out of nothing, as in creation, Only God can sustain and renew life on this planet. Only God can act globally in restraining evil and convicting men of sin. All these things are said to be done by the Holy Spirit. The Holy Spirit has had an active relationship with this world from the very beginning.

- **He was active in creating the world**, "and the Spirit of God was hovering over the waters." (Gen 1:2, see also Psa 33:6).
- **He is active in renewing the world**. What we call the 'law of nature' is really the activity of the Holy Spirit, "When you send your Spirit, they are created, and you renew the face of the ground." (Psa 104:29-30).
- **He was active in restraining evil**, "Then the LORD said, "My Spirit will not contend with humans forever,"" (Gen 6:3, see also 2 The 2:7).
- **He is active in convicting men of sin**, "he will prove the world to be in the wrong about sin and righteousness and judgement:" (Jhn 16:8).

The Spirit in the Old Testament

The Old Testament shows us an activity of the Holy Spirit which is very wonderful. The Spirit was the source of special abilities that were given to God's servants to enable them to do supernatural things. He filled with wisdom the craftsmen employed in building the Tabernacle, "See, the LORD has chosen Bezalel ... and he has filled him with the Spirit of God, with wisdom, with understanding, with knowledge and with all kinds of skills" (Exo 35:30-31). The Spirit came upon Joshua and filled him with wisdom for leadership, "Now Joshua son of Nun was filled with the spirit of wisdom because Moses had laid his hands on him." (Deu 34:9). So too, in the book of Judges, we see that men were raised up and empowered by the Spirit to deliver Israel from her enemies, "The Spirit of the LORD came on him (Othniel), so that he became Israel's judge" (Jdg 3:10); "The Spirit of the LORD came powerfully upon him (Samson) so that he tore the lion apart with his bare hands" (Jdg 14:6).

The long line of prophets spoke "by the Spirit" (2 Pet 1:21). Their prophetic messages contained two important predictions about a future age. Firstly, that Messiah would come, a man from God, endowed with the Spirit in the fullest way, "The Spirit of the LORD will rest on him" (Isa 11:2); "Here is my servant, whom I uphold, my chosen one in whom I delight; I will put my Spirit on him," (Isa 42:1). Secondly, that the Spirit would be poured out upon all peoples, "And afterward, I will pour out my Spirit on all people ... Even on my servants, both men and women, I will pour out my Spirit in those days." (Joe 2:28-29).

✎ Assignment

Take one character from the Old Testament and show how the Holy Spirit enabled him to fulfil his calling from God.

The Holy Spirit in the life of Christ

During the time of Christ's ministry on earth, the Holy Spirit anointed him, and worked through him, in a unique way. Jesus was 'Messiah', God's anointed one, who was endowed with the fullness of the Spirit. Jesus saw his ministry as a fulfilment of the Old Testament prophecy

"The Spirit of the Lord is on me, because he has anointed me to proclaim good news to the poor. He has sent me to proclaim freedom for the prisoners and recovery of sight for the blind, to set the oppressed free, to proclaim the year of the Lord's favour." (Luk 4:18-19).

- **Christ's birth was made possible by the Spirit**, "This is how the birth of Jesus the Messiah came about: His mother Mary was pledged to be married to Joseph, but before they came together, she was found to be pregnant through the Holy Spirit." (Mat 1:18,20).
- **Christ was empowered by the Spirit at his baptism**, "and the Holy Spirit descended on him in bodily form like a dove." (Luk 3:22, see also Luk 4:1).
- **Christ claimed the fulfilment of Isa 61:1**, which spoke of Messiah being anointed by the Spirit in a unique way, "He began by saying to them, "Today this scripture is fulfilled in your hearing" (Luk 4:18-21).
- **The miraculous ministry of Christ** was carried out through the power of the Spirit, "how God anointed Jesus of Nazareth with the Holy Spirit and power, and how he went around doing good and healing all who were under the power of the devil, because God was with him." (Act 10:38).
- **Christ cast out evil spirits by the Holy Spirit**, "But if I drive out demons by the finger of God, then the kingdom of God has come upon you." (Luk 11:20).
- **In his death Christ made an offering of himself to God by the Spirit**, "How much more, then, will the blood of Christ, who through the eternal Spirit offered himself unblemished to God," (Heb 9:14).
- **When Jesus ascended to the right hand of God**, he sent the Holy Spirit to his followers, "Exalted to the right hand of God, he has received from the Father the promised Holy Spirit and has poured out what you now see and hear." (Act 2:33).

Assignment

In which ways was the Lord Jesus dependant on the Holy Spirit to fulfil his mission in the world.

The Holy Spirit in the New Testament

The very same Spirit that anointed Christ has been given to believers, that we might live out the life of Christ in this world. When Jesus spoke of sending the Holy Spirit to his disciples, he promised to send, "another advocate to help you and be with you forever--" (Jhn 14:16). This word 'another' does not signify one of another kind, but one of the same kind as himself. The Spirit is of the same nature as Christ.

The Holy Spirit has come to fill the place that Jesus occupied in the lives of his disciples. He comes to believers as their teacher, guide, counsellor and comforter. He is the empowering presence of God in all who receive him.

> *The Holy Spirit is the empowering presence of God in all who receive him.*

The day of Pentecost saw the fulfilment of the promise of Jesus to his disciples, (Act 2). This was the birthday of the church.

The whole Redemptive plan of God, bought with the blood of Jesus, was to be carried forward by the personal presence and anointing of the Holy Spirit upon believers.

The Spirit gave the believers boldness to witness, "And they were all filled with the Holy Spirit and spoke the word of God boldly." (Act 4:31-33). The leaders were enabled to perform wonders and signs, by the power of the Holy Spirit, "The apostles performed many signs and wonders among the people." (Act 5:12). Those same believers became a temple for God to dwell in, "And in him you too are being built together to become a dwelling in which God lives by his Spirit." (Eph 2:22).

The work of the Spirit in believers

The Holy Spirit works in the lives of God's people in a special way. He comes in a most intimate way to dwell in, and work through them. He is the one who quickens new life in them, and fills them with power to live for Christ. He seals up the work of redemption in their hearts, marking them as God's own people. They are utterly dependant on the Spirit for every sanctifying grace, for their hearts to be made pure.

The Holy Spirit has come as the down-payment, or foretaste of our future inheritance, "When you believed, you were marked in him with a seal, the promised Holy Spirit, who is **a deposit guaranteeing our inheritance** until the redemption of those who are God's possession--to the praise of his glory." (Eph 1:13-14). This means that the coming of the Holy Spirit relates to our inheritance in the Kingdom of God. Through the Holy Spirit's presence, and anointing, believers are to 'taste of the powers of the age to come'. When Paul said "For the kingdom of God is not a matter of eating and drinking, but of righteousness, peace and joy in the Holy Spirit," (Rom 14:17), he was linking the coming of the Spirit with our experience of the Kingdom of God in this life.

- **The Holy Spirit gives new life to believers**, "The wind blows wherever it pleases ... So it is with everyone born of the Spirit." (Jhn 3:8).

- **The Holy Spirit comes to fill believers**, "All of them were filled with the Holy Spirit and began to speak in other tongues" (Act 2:4).

- **The Holy Spirit comes to seal believers**, putting his mark of ownership upon them, "When you believed, you were marked in him with a seal, the promised Holy Spirit," (Eph 1:13).

- **The Holy Spirit inspires prophecy**, (1 Cor 14:29-30 cp. 1 Cor 12:7)

- **The Holy Spirit sanctifies believers**, "so that the Gentiles might become an offering acceptable to God, sanctified by the Holy Spirit." (Rom 15:6).

- **The Holy Spirit gives gifts to believers**, "Now to each one the manifestation of the Spirit is given for the common good." (1 Cor 12:7-10).

- **The Holy Spirit brings assurance of sonship to believers**, "the Spirit you received brought about your adoption to sonship. And by him we cry, '*Abba*, Father.'" (Rom 8:15).

- **The Holy Spirit comes to teach believers**, "But the Advocate, the Holy Spirit, whom the Father will send in my name, will teach you all things and will remind you of everything I have said to you." (Jhn 14:26)

- **The Holy Spirit comes to guide believers**, "But when he, the Spirit of truth, comes, he will guide you into all the truth." (Jhn 16:13).

- **The Holy Spirit comes to intercede**, "but the Spirit himself intercedes for us through wordless groans." (Rom 8:26-27).

- **The Holy Spirit puts glory on believers**, "Now the Lord is the Spirit, and where the Spirit of the Lord is, there is freedom. And we all, who with unveiled faces contemplate the Lord's glory, are being transformed into his image with ever-increasing glory, which comes from the Lord, who is the Spirit." (2 Cor 3:17-18).

"Pentecost challenges the very citadel of our faith. The gift of the Spirit is a distinguishing feature of the Christian religion. It is the very soul of our faith. In his indwelling presence is the secret of all Christian experience, and in the abiding energy of his power is the dynamic of all Christian service."

- Chadwick 'The way to Pentecost' p. 117

✎ Assignment
What are some of the special works of the Holy Spirit in the life of believers?

Notes

God's Eternal Purpose

Study 7
The Doctrine of the Kingdom of God

📖 **Matthew 5:1-16**

Introduction

The Kingdom of God is a major theme that runs through all the pages of Holy Scripture. It is possibly the one theme that links all the revelation of the Bible together. Over the years there has been many differing views, expressed by various Christian groups, regarding the Kingdom of God. Some groups have concentrated on the Kingdom being expressed in this age through the arena of politics. They have used this ideology to put forward political and social ideas to try and change society for the better. Other groups have seen the Kingdom belonging entirely to the future, when Christ comes again. Within this group the 'Dispensationalists' have given prominence to the position of Israel during a future Millennial reign of Messiah in Jerusalem. More recently a more balanced view has been emerging, which speaks of the Kingdom of God as already present in the earth, but which looks to the actual return of Christ to bring the Kingdom to its fullness.

What we will do in this study is look at the nature and purpose of the Kingdom of God and how it progressively comes to its fulfilment in the person of Christ.

"The Biblical idea of the Kingdom of God is deeply rooted in the Old Testament and is grounded in the confidence that there is one eternal, living God who has revealed himself to men and who has a purpose for the human race which he has chosen to accomplish through Israel. The Biblical hope is therefore a religious hope; it is an essential element in the revealed will and the redemptive work of the living God."

- Eldon Ladd 'The Gospel of the Kingdom' p.14

What is the Kingdom?

The Greek word for kingdom *basileia* should not be thought of primarily as a realm over which a sovereign rules, e.g. The United Kingdom of Great Britain. The word focuses on the rule of the King himself and could be translated 'Kingship' or 'Royal Dominion'. The term 'Kingdom of God' is really speaking of the Kingship or Rule of God. Where that rule is accepted blessing and righteousness is expressed, and people are brought into the salvation of God.

God as King

The Kingship of God 'Yahweh' is revealed at different levels in the Scriptures:

1. God is King of all creation
2. God is King of the world
3. God is King of Israel

God is King of all creation

God's rule is absolute. He is King of both men and angelic beings, "The LORD has established his throne in heaven, and his kingdom rules over all. Praise the LORD, you his angels, you mighty ones who do his bidding, who obey his word. Praise the LORD, all his heavenly hosts, you his servants who do his will. Praise the LORD, all his works everywhere in his dominion. Praise the LORD, my soul." (Psa 103:19-22). The glory and permanence of this kingdom is expressed in the Psalms, "They tell of the glory of your kingdom and speak of your might, so that all people may know of your mighty Act and the glorious splendour of your kingdom. Your kingdom is an everlasting kingdom, and your dominion endures through all generations." (Psa 145:10-13). Again, "The LORD is King for ever and ever;" (Psa 10:16).

God is King of the world

Many of the Psalms pick up on the Kingship of God and God's reign over the earth "For the LORD Most High is awesome, the great King over all the earth." (Psa 47:2). The word that Daniel spoke to king Nebuchadnezzar in the interpretation of a dream shows the same truth, "until you acknowledge that the Most High is sovereign over all kingdoms on earth and gives them to anyone he wishes." (Dan 4:25) Paul expressed a similar thought when he said, "for there is no authority except that which God has established." (Rom 13:1).

God is King of Israel

Following the fall of Adam, from his high position under God, the world rebels against the rule of Yahweh. In order that his kingly rights over the world could be demonstrated, God chose the nation of Israel to come under his authority. This was expressed in the form of a covenant. Israel was destined to come under the saving rule of God, but she rejected that rule and called for an earthly king, "And the LORD told him: "Listen to all that the people are saying to you; it is not you they have rejected, but they have rejected me as their king." (1 Sam 8:7). However, God used the office of king in Israel to show that he was still sovereign, "This is what the LORD says-- Israel's King and Redeemer, the LORD Almighty: I am the first and I am the last; apart from me there is no God." (Isa 44:6).

✎ Assignment
If God is King of the earth why are there so many problems in the world?

The under-lordship of this world

The Sovereign creator decided to express his rule over planet earth in a special way, through a created being. God put Adam and Eve in a position of trust when he made them in his image. An essential part of that God-likeness was the expression of lordship through man. The account of creation in Genesis shows how God gave dominion over the whole of life on earth to Adam, "God blessed them and said to them, 'Rule over the fish in the sea and the birds in the sky and over every living creature that moves on the ground.'" (Gen 1:28).

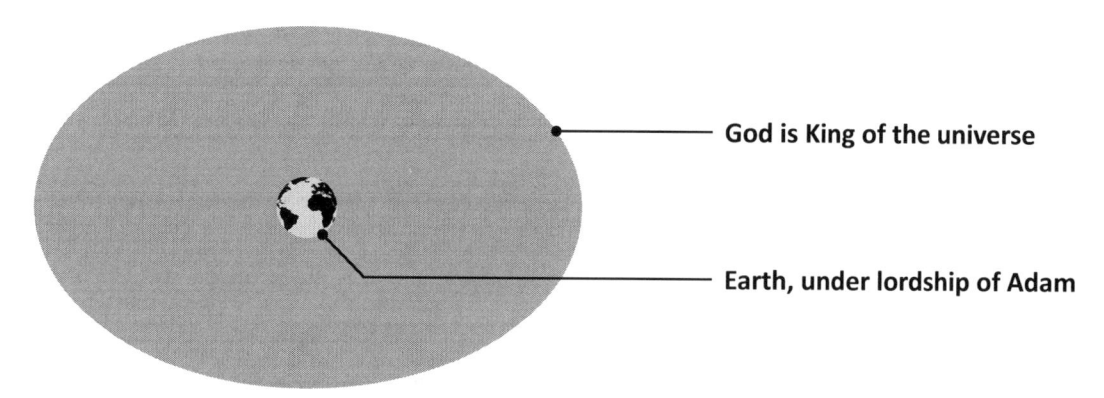

God is King of the universe

Earth, under lordship of Adam

This lordship of Adam was also shown when God brought the animals to him to name them. In this way Adam showed his authority over them, "He brought them to the man to see what he would name them; and whatever the man called each living creature, that was its name." (Gen 2:19). Similarly, the absolute Lord-ship of God was shown when he called things into being and then named them, "God called the light 'day,' and the darkness he called 'night.'" (Gen 1:5, see also Gen 1: 8,10). In this way God was revealing his absolute authority over our solar system, and that he had the right to intervene in his creation as he willed. This sovereign rule was expressed over the whole universe as God called stars into being and named them, "He determines the number of the stars and calls them each by name." (Psa 147:4).

Adam fails the test

The tragedy of Adam and Eve's failure went far beyond their personal sin. The consequences were enormous for the whole human race. Adam stood, not just as an individual in his relationship with God, but as the head of the whole human race. What Adam did, for good or bad, affected all his descendants. In listening to the voice of the serpent, Adam chose to obey the word of Satan rather than the word of God. In doing that he surrendered his under-lordship of the world to Satan and entered into a relationship with him. Isaiah brought out the consequences of this in his day, "You boast, 'We have entered into a covenant with death, with the realm of the dead we have made an agreement'." (Isa 28:15). From that time on Satan became the ruler of this world, "and that the whole world is under the control of the evil one" (1 Jhn 5:19). Satan's objective was to hold men and women in darkness and unbelief toward God, "The god of this age has blinded the minds of unbelievers, so that they cannot see the light of the gospel that displays the glory of Christ," (2 Cor 4:4).

✎ Assignment
What are some of the effects of Adams failure upon mankind's relationship with God?

Recovery in the plan of God

As a consequence of Adam's failure, all humanity has been born in a system under Satan, with no hope, and no ability to break through the system. Paul says, "you were dead in your transgressions and sins ... when you followed the ways of this world and of the ruler of the kingdom of the air, the spirit who is now at work in those who are disobedient. Like the rest, we were by nature deserving of wrath." (Eph 2:1-3). God was still sovereign and could intervene in this world, so why did he not simply destroy the devil? If God had destroyed Satan for his rebellion, he would have been committed to destroying Adam and Eve for their rebellion. God had a higher plan, and in that plan all creatures with a moral capacity must be tested to show their willing allegiance to him. It seems that God allowed sin in heaven among the angels in order to test their allegiance. The result of that testing was that many of them followed the rebellion of Satan.

For the image of God in Adam to come to its proper destiny, his character had to be tested. God wanted a special relationship with mankind that would come freely from our deepest will. When Adam fell into sin, it ruined God's plan in creation. However, hidden in the depths of God was his plan of restoration for all nations, through redemption, "Now to him who is able to establish you in accordance with my gospel, the message I proclaim about Jesus Christ, in keeping with the revelation of the mystery hidden for long ages past, but now revealed and made known through the prophetic writings by the command of the eternal God, so that all the Gentiles might come to the obedience that comes from faith-- to the only wise God be glory forever through Jesus Christ! Amen." (Rom 16:25-27). In the great mystery of these events God was able to make a greater revelation of himself. If Adam had never failed there would never have been a revelation of the amazing grace and mercy of God. God allowed the tragedy of the fall of mankind and the opposition of Satan. In all the resulting catastrophe God has revealed himself as the God of salvation and restoration. This is nothing less than the outworking of God's eternal purpose.

> *Hidden in the depths of God was his plan of restoration for all nations, through redemption.*

God's Redemptive Kingdom in the Old Testament

God continued to express absolute Lordship even after the fall of Adam. He indicated to the serpent (the devil) that his downfall would be brought about, and that mankind would know a deliverer, "And I will put enmity between you and the woman, and between your offspring and hers; he will crush your head, and you will strike his heel." (Gen 3:15). God is perfect. However, every expression of his Kingdom throughout the Old Testament, was made imperfect through the fallenness of mankind. The Old Testament shows how mankind divided between those who acknowledge God, such as Abel, Enoch and Noah, and those who rejected him, such as Cain and Lamech. The result of Adam's rebellion began to fill the earth, "The

LORD saw how great the wickedness of the human race had become on the earth, and that every inclination of the thoughts of the human heart was only evil all the time." (Gen 6:5). God, in his sovereignty, brought judgement upon all peoples, "So the LORD said, 'I will wipe from the face of the earth the human race I have created ... for I regret that I have made them.' But Noah found favour in the eyes of the LORD." (Gen 6:7-8). In accord with his salvation plan God saved Noah and began again.

God chose Abraham and tested him in a very great way, that through him he might bring to birth a nation who would live under the rule of God, "The LORD had said to Abram, 'Go from your country, your people and your father's household to the land I will show you. I will make you into a great nation, and I will bless you; I will make your name great, and you will be a blessing'." (Gen 12:1-2). In the story of Israel there are tiny glimpses of the Kingdom of God, but always within the brokenness of life. Israel itself was broken and could not keep the law of God or reveal the rule of God in an acceptable way.

What became clear is that, unless God intervened in a very direct way, his kingly rule would never be expressed in a way that allowed his will to be "done on earth as it is in heaven".

Two things emerge very clearly from the stories and revelations of the Old Testament:

1. That all mankind needed to be restored to a right relationship with God, because all sinned and needed salvation.
2. That the way of salvation was through Redemption and Atonement, which involved sacrifice and the shedding of blood.

The coming of Jesus Christ

In the coming of Jesus the Christ, the Kingly rule of God began to be expressed in a far greater way. This was because, for the first time since Adam failed, there was a perfect man on earth who was under the full authority of God. God the Father could express his rule perfectly through the person of Jesus Christ his Son, even though it was expressed within the brokenness of life. Satan was still active, mankind was still rebellious and there were huge problems that needed to be dealt with before the new order of the Kingdom of God could be fully restored.

The ministry and teaching of Christ was almost exclusively taken up with the Kingdom of God. Only twice he mentioned the Church, (Mat 16:18 & Mat 18:17).

The man Christ Jesus needed to take back the rights of under-lordship, which were initially given to Adam, and surrendered to Satan. In the life of Christ, in the gospels, there was a fierce battle between Christ and Satan. This was shown in the account of the temptation of Christ in the wilderness, (Luk 4:1-13). It was there that Christ dismissed the onslaught of Satan by expressing his trust in the Word of God, "It is written". In one of the temptations Satan offered

The man Christ Jesus needed to take back the rights of under-lordship which were initially given to Adam, and surrendered to Satan.

God's Eternal Purpose: An introduction to Christian doctrine

to Christ "all the kingdoms of the world," on the basis that they belonged to him by right, "I will give you all their authority and splendour; it has been given to me, and I can give it to anyone I want to." (Luk 4:5-6).

However, Christ was intent on gaining that authority by a different means, in which the power of Satan would be broken, and a multitude of mankind delivered. Satan had successfully tempted Eve into grasping after a position that was not given to her. She had been made in the image of God, but Satan suggested that she could be equal with God, (Gen 3:5). In the wilderness temptation, Christ, who was equal with God, "made himself nothing by taking the very nature of a servant" (Phi 2:6). It was in that lowly state that Christ overcame the tempters power.

The battle against the despotic rule of Satan, and its consequences for mankind, was also displayed through Christ in his breaking the power of sickness. Sometimes he cast sickness out of a whole region showing both his compassion and his Lordship, "They ran throughout that whole region and carried the sick on mats to wherever they heard he was. And wherever he went--into villages, towns or countryside--they placed the sick in the marketplaces. They begged him to let them touch even the edge of his cloak, and all who touched it were healed." (Mar 6:53-56). Peter testified to Cornelius and his family "how God anointed Jesus of Nazareth with the Holy Spirit and power, and how he went around doing good and healing all who were under the power of the devil, because God was with him." (Act 10:38).

Christ revealed his Lordship over nature, when he calmed the storm, "He got up, rebuked the wind and said to the waves, 'Quiet! Be still!' Then the wind died down and it was completely calm." (Mar 4:39). That same Lordship was displayed when he walked on the water. Christ exercised an authority that was greater than the laws of nature, "Shortly before dawn Jesus went out to them, walking on the lake. When the disciples saw him walking on the lake, they were terrified." (Mat 14:25-26).

The Lordship of Christ was further displayed when he cast out demons. Those evil spirits, under the lordship of Satan, were subject to the authority of Christ, "But if it is by the Spirit of God that I drive out demons, then the kingdom of God has come upon you." (Mat 12:28).

Christ displayed his Lordship over death itself, showing that he had authority to reverse the direct consequences of the fall of Adam, including the judgement of death which was past upon him. This was revealed in the raising of Lazarus, even after he had been dead for four days, (Jhn 11:1-44). Jesus showed Martha that he had power from God to raise the dead; in the way some had been raised from the dead in the Old Testament. He also showed that he himself was the resurrection and the Life, "Martha answered, 'I know he will rise again in the resurrection at the last day'". (Jhn 11:24).

"Jesus said to her, 'I am the resurrection and the life. The one who believes in me will live, even though they die'" (Jhn 11:25).

Through the strength of his sinless righteousness, Christ gained supremacy over Satan, "I will not say much more to you, for the prince of this world is coming. He has no hold over me," (Jhn 14:30).

In his death and resurrection, Christ paid the price for sinners to be forgiven. He made a way, for all who looked to him, to come under his rule in the Kingdom of God, and escape from under the rule of Satan, "For he has rescued us from the dominion of darkness and brought us into the kingdom of the Son he loves," (Col 1:13). In his resurrection Christ displayed his total victory over sin, Satan and death.

"And it was essential ... that he should rise from the dead and thereby confirm not only his total conquest of sin and death and the overthrow of their dread reign but also the rebirth of our race in himself, the last Adam."

- Edgecumbe Hughes, 'The True Image' p.134

In Christ's death and resurrection he guaranteed the total victory of the Kingdom that he announced and displayed in his life. That Kingdom must prevail over every power on earth or under the earth. It must increase against every opposition, until the earth is subdued under Christ's feet, "Of the greatness of his government and peace there will be no end. He will reign on David's throne and over his kingdom, establishing and upholding it with justice and righteousness from that time on and forever. The zeal of the LORD Almighty will accomplish this." (Isa 9:7). Paul expressed confidence in the fact of Christ's supremacy, displayed in the resurrection, when he said, "For he must reign until he has put all his enemies under his feet." (1 Cor 15:25).

Assignment
In which ways did Christ show his supremacy over Satan?

The Kingdom of God present and future

Unless we see the tension in Scripture, with regard to the Kingdom of God being 'now and not yet', we will struggle to understand what is being said. For example, Paul states, "For the kingdom of God is not a matter of eating and drinking, but of righteousness, peace and joy in the Holy Spirit," (Rom 14:17). Paul is clearly teaching that these attributes should be manifested in the lives of believers, in this life. On the other hand, Jesus said, said,

"Then the King will say to those on his right, 'Come, you who are blessed by my Father; take your inheritance, the kingdom prepared for you since the creation of the world'". (Mat 25:34). Here it clearly indicates that the Kingdom is a future inheritance that God will bestow upon his people when Christ returns in glory.

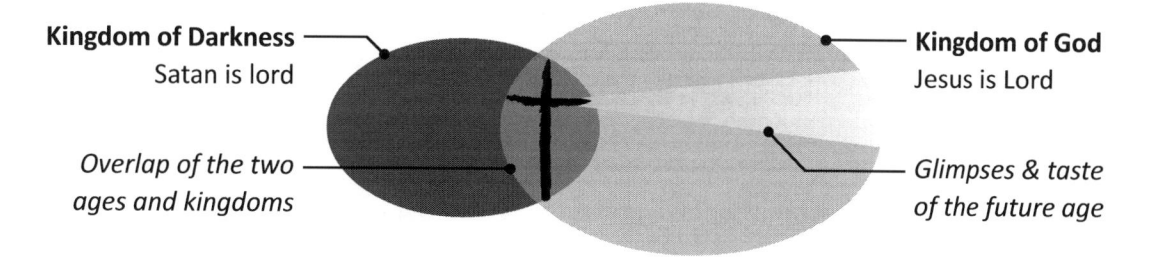

Kingdom of Darkness — Satan is lord

Kingdom of God — Jesus is Lord

Overlap of the two ages and kingdoms

Glimpses & taste of the future age

Again, the Scriptures speak of the Kingdom as a realm into which believers enter now. Jesus said, "The Law and the Prophets were proclaimed until John. Since that time, the good news of the kingdom of God is being preached, and everyone is forcing their way into it." (Luk 16:16). Those who respond to the message and person of Christ are those who are already pressing into the Kingdom.

There are other Scriptures which describe the Kingdom in terms of a future realm which Christians, will enter at Christ's return. For example, Peter writes, "and you will receive a rich welcome into the eternal kingdom of our Lord and Saviour Jesus Christ." (2 Pet 1:11). Or the words of Jesus, "The Son of Man will send out his angels, and they will weed out of his kingdom everything that causes sin and all who do evil. They will throw them into the blazing furnace, where there will be weeping ... Then the righteous will shine like the sun in the kingdom of their Father. Whoever has ears, let them hear." (Mat 13:41,43).

The apostolic gospel

Since Christ's ministry and teaching was largely taken up with presenting the Kingdom of God, why is it that so little of 'the Kingdom' is taught in the letters of the apostles? It is not that they say nothing about it, "For two whole years Paul stayed there in his own rented house and welcomed all who came to see him. He proclaimed the kingdom of God and taught about the Lord Jesus Christ--with all boldness and without hindrance!" (Act 28:30-31). Paul tells us something of the real nature of the Kingdom of God expressed now, "For the kingdom of God is not a matter of talk but of power." (1 Cor 4:20). However, the apostolic writings do not give the same prominence to the Kingdom of God that Jesus gave. Why is this? It seems that the apostles majored on the truth of the Lordship of Christ. The central issue, regarding Christ's authority to bring people into the Kingdom rule of God, was that he, and not Satan, was Lord. The transcendent truth to the apostles was that Jesus of Nazareth was both 'Lord and Christ', "Therefore let all Israel be assured of this: God has made this Jesus, whom you crucified, both Lord (sovereign) and Messiah (God's anointed king)." (Act 2:36).

The glorious truth taught by the apostles is that Jesus is both Sovereign Lord of all (and sits on his Fathers throne) and the under-Lord of the earth (and sits on the throne of this world). As Jesus himself said, "To the one who is victorious, I will give the right to sit with me on my throne, just as I was victorious and sat down with my Father on his throne." (Rev 3:21). Those who overcome the 'spirit of this age' are linked with the throne of Christ over this world. An essential part of the restored image of God in believers must be the restoration of kingdom authority. Whilst it can only be expressed in its fullness after the return of Christ, the foretaste of the age to come is granted to us in the Kingdom now.

The Christian life begins with a submission to the Lordship of Christ, "If you declare with your mouth, '**Jesus is Lord**,' and believe in your heart that God raised him from the dead, you will be saved." (Rom 10:9). In response to the Philippian jailer's question "Sirs, what must I do to be saved" Paul and Silas replied, "Believe in the **Lord Jesus Christ**, and you will be saved" (Act 16:30-31). After the initial confession, all growth and development in the life of the believer is about applying the Lordship of Christ to every part of life. This is a learning process.

Paul's prayer and vision for the saints is clearly stated in Ephesians, and he links all the revelation of God's purpose for his people to the exalted position of Christ as Lord. "For this reason, ever since I heard about your faith in the Lord Jesus and your love for all God's people, I have not stopped giving thanks for you, remembering you in my prayers. I keep asking that the God of our Lord Jesus Christ, the glorious Father, may give you the Spirit of wisdom and revelation, so that you may know him better. I pray that the eyes of your heart may be enlightened in order that you may know the hope to which he has called you, the riches of his glorious inheritance in his holy people, and his incomparably great power for us who believe. That power is the same as the mighty strength he exerted when he raised Christ from the dead and seated him at his right hand in the heavenly realms, far above all rule and authority, power and dominion, and every name that is invoked, not only in the present age but also in the one to come. And God placed all things under his feet and appointed him to be head over everything for the church, which is his body, the fullness of him who fills everything in every way." (Eph 1:15-23).

Christ's Lordship over believers

It is through our submission to Christ as Lord that the Kingdom of God will be manifested through us. Christ continues to express his authority over the effects of the fall of mankind. Sickness and demons are still to be challenged, through faith in the Lordship of Christ. We are intended to 'taste the power of the coming age' (Heb 6:4). Christ promised his followers, "To the one who is victorious and does my will to the end, I will give authority over the nations--" (Rev 2:26). The foretaste of that authority is to be expressed through the gospel of the kingdom. God's people can carry an authority in Christ that affects the destiny of nations. Through prayers of faith and the proclamation of God's truth the 'kingdoms of this world' are impacted by the Kingdom of God. In the past the church has known times of great progress and power, and also times of regress and defeat. The issue facing every generation of the church is how much it will come under Christ's Lordship, and how much it will manifest his life.

Assignment
In which ways can the believer experience the Kingdom of God in this life?

The Kingdom and the Church

The truth that believers are to continue the ministry of Christ in the world is conveyed through the church being called 'the body of Christ'. In this way the Church becomes the means, in God's hands, of carrying the gospel of the kingdom that Christ initiated and bought with his own blood. The Church bears witness to the victory of Christ over Satan and, with faith in Christ's Lordship speaks deliverance into the brokenness of life. Whilst the Kingdom of God is bigger than the Church, it is the Church that must be seen as the main instrument through which God carries forward his purpose in the world.

Conclusion

The whole of the created order heads towards a destiny where the Lordship of Christ will be acknowledged. "Therefore God exalted him to the highest place and gave him the name that is above every name, that at the name of Jesus every knee should bow, in heaven and on earth and under the earth, and every tongue acknowledge that Jesus Christ is Lord, to the glory of God the Father." (Phi 2:9-11)

This great event will take place after the Coming of Christ and the resurrection of believers. God's original purpose, for the whole of creation, was that it would come under the absolute rule of his Son. "He made known to us the mystery of his will according to his good pleasure, which he purposed in Christ, to be put into effect when the times reach their fulfilment--to bring unity to all things in heaven and on earth under Christ." (Eph 1:9-10). Only in this way can creation find the fulfilment of the purpose for which it was made. It was for this purpose that the Son of God became incarnate and gave his all as an atoning sacrifice. As a prelude to the whole universe being restored to its intended order and purpose, the people of God are to be shown as a kind of first-fruits, "For the creation waits in eager expectation for the children of God to be revealed." (Rom 8:19). The glory of Redemption that is to be revealed, in the once ruined 'sons of God', will be a sign to all creation that its purpose and glory is secured by the same Redemptive sacrifice of Christ. It is the foretaste of all this that has been given to the people of God. The coming of the Holy Spirit as the deposit or down payment of our future inheritance, (Eph 1:14), is something far more glorious than the Church comprehends.

When all these things are fulfilled, Christ will hand the Kingdom authority back to the Father who gave it to him, "Then the end will come, when he hands over the kingdom to God the Father after he has destroyed all dominion, authority and power. For he must reign until he has put all his enemies under his feet." (1 Cor 15:24-28). This is as far as the revelation of Scripture takes us. We cannot see beyond this point, but we anticipate something utterly glorious in the Kingdom of God.

Notes

God's Eternal Purpose

Study 8

The Doctrine of the Church

📖 **1 Corinthians 12:12-31**

Introduction

Over the years the term 'church' has, for many, lost its original meaning. We refer to a denominational organisation as a church. We speak of a building used for religious purposes as a church. We refer to a religious service or ceremony as church. These meanings were never intended by Scripture, and none of them gives insight into the New Testament idea of what the Church of Jesus Christ is.

What is the church?

The word 'church' is the translation of the Greek word *ecclesia*. In the first century the word was used to indicate an official summoning of the citizens of a Greek city state to a meeting to discuss public affairs. Hence, they were 'the called out ones', which is the basic meaning behind the word *ecclesia*. The word was adopted by the Christian community to show that they were called out of their idolatrous and immoral ways, to form a unique company of God's people. They formed a new community or 'congregation' which was committed to the person and teaching of Jesus Christ and the spread of his gospel.

They were separated from the world, not by the walls of a monastery, nor by segregation from other people, but by a life style of true holiness and devotion to Christ.

The great truths regarding the Church were only made known after the resurrection of Christ. The New Testament Church began at Pentecost, with the coming of the Spirit. However, the full purpose of God is made up of all true believers, throughout time, including both the Old and New Testament. Jesus committed himself to the task of building his church against all opposition, "and on this rock I will build my church, and the gates of Hades will not overcome it." (Mat 16:18). The ultimate purpose for which Christ died was to have a 'called out' people of his own, his *ecclesia*, "just as Christ loved the church and gave himself up for her" (Eph 5:25).

In the New Testament the word 'church' was sometimes used of small groups of believers meeting in a home, "Greet also the church that meets at their house." (Rom 16:5). It was also used to denote a large company of believers living in a whole city, such as Jerusalem, even if they met in separate homes, "News of this reached the church in Jerusalem" (Act 11:22). And also to Corinth, "To the church of God in Corinth," (1 Cor 1:2). It was also used, in the plural form ,to indicate believers in a whole region or nation, "To the churches in Galatia:" (Gal 1:2). When no location was specified the word 'Church' referred to the world wide body of believers.

Christ and the church

There are only two occasions recorded in the gospels in which Christ spoke of the church. The first was concerning the universal church, which was to be built on the confession of Jesus as the Christ, the Son of God, "on this rock I will build my church," (Mat 16:18). The second was giving advice to the local church on how to handle problems, "If they still refuse to listen, tell it to the church;" (Mat 18:17).

From the record that we have, the idea of the church did not figure prominently in the teaching of Christ. He came to establish the kingdom of God, which was to make way for the formation of the church. Nevertheless, after Peter's confession of him, Jesus said "On this rock I will build my church". In this statement Jesus was recognising the disciples as the first small *ecclesia*.

The Church is chosen in Christ

The church, in its origin and purpose, is from God. It is planned in and through Christ, "he made known to us the mystery of his will according to his good pleasure, which he purposed in Christ, to be put into effect when the times reach their fulfilment--to bring unity to all things in heaven and on earth under Christ." (Eph 1:9-10).

The Church is not a social organisation designed merely to help people at an intellectual or emotional level. Membership of the church is not by human appointment, but by God's initiative, "For we know, brothers and sisters loved by God, that he has chosen you, because our gospel came to you not simply with words but also with power, with the Holy Spirit and deep conviction." (1 The 1:4-5).

This raises the whole question of election, and the remarkable grace of God from which it springs. From all eternity God has purposed to reveal his image in a part of his creation. Then, to link that creation with himself in outworking a plan that expresses his heart. It seemed as if that plan of God was ruined by the fall of Adam and the usurpation of lordship rights over the world by Satan. However, God was not taken by surprise. In Christ he chose a people for himself who would be restored to his favour and purpose. Some aspects of God's election are beyond our understanding, but Scripture gives us some insights into the heart of God regarding this matter.

- **Election comes out of the love of God and leads to sonship** – "In love he predestined us for adoption to sonship through Jesus Christ," (Eph 1:5)
- **Election is according to the plan and will of God** – "In him we were also chosen, having been predestined according to the plan of him who works out everything in

conformity with the purpose of his will," (Eph 1:11)

- **Election is in accord with the foreknowledge of God and leads to obedience to Christ** – "who have been chosen according to the foreknowledge of God the Father, through the sanctifying work of the Spirit, to be obedient to Jesus Christ and sprinkled with his blood:" (1 Pet 1:2).
- **Election is a reason for praising God** – "But we ought always to thank God for you, brothers and sisters loved by the Lord, because God chose you as firstfruits to be saved through the sanctifying work of the Spirit" (2 The 2:13).

Marks of a true church

The gathered church is sometimes made up of a mixture of believers and unbelievers. Paul had to warn Timothy of the effect of false brothers bringing bad teaching into the church, (2 Tim 2:17-18). Paul also warned the church at Ephesus that after he had departed, "savage wolves will come in among you and will not spare the flock." (Act 20:29-30). The Lord showed, in his parables of the Kingdom, how Satan would plant tares among the wheat. Both were to be left to grow until the harvest, when the angels would separate them, (Mat 13:24-30). This does not mean that the church accepts just anyone as a member of the body of Christ. Although non-believers are to be welcomed to the public meetings of the church, they should not be regarded as a part of the church until they come to a commitment of faith in the Lordship of Christ. A distinction must be made between the people of God and the people of this world, or the Church will face all kinds of unnecessary problems. The early church called for a confession of faith, such as "Jesus is Lord" (1 Cor 12:3), to be made at baptism, (see also Act 8:37).

In the past the church was defined by the Roman Catholic view, which saw the church having a physical link with the apostle Peter. This was supposedly achieved through bishops being ordained by other bishops, who could trace their ordination back to Peter. Peter was believed to be the first Pope, and ordained by Christ. Therefore, each 'true church' had to be under the rule of an ordained bishop, through the lineage of the apostle Peter. The Reformers of the sixteenth century, by contrast, said;

"Wherever we see the Word of God sincerely preached and heard, wherever we see the sacraments administered according to the institution of Christ, there we cannot have any doubt that the Church of God has some existence"

- Calvin 'Institutes of the Christian Religion' Vol 4, 1.9

I would add two things which are necessary for the church to function in the New Testament sense. Firstly, there must be an ordained leadership, and secondly there must be the known presence of the Spirit of God.

Assignment
What are the essential features to be found in a true church?

The analogies used to describe the Church

The New Testament portrays the Church, and its ministry, through the use of different analogies. It is **'a body'** - for Christ to express himself through; **'a building'** - for God to dwell in; **'a family'** - to reveal relationship; **'a bride'** - to show love at its deepest level; **'a foundation of truth'** - to show stability.

The church as a body

This remarkable analogy shows us the closeness of our union with Christ. The Son of God has ordained to indwell his people, by his Spirit, to form a body, "the glorious riches of this mystery, which is Christ in you, the hope of glory." (Col 1:27). As head of the body he lives out his life in, and through, his people. The church is the physical representation of Christ on earth; we are his hands and his feet, members of his body.

> *The analogy of the Church as the body of Christ shows us that believers are linked as an organism and share the life of Christ.*

The analogy of the church as the body of Christ shows us that believers are linked as an organism and share the life of Christ through a loving relationship with one another. That body is also to reveal the heart of Christ to a needy world.

- **Members of the body of Christ have different gifts** (1 Cor 12:4-27).

- **Members of the body of Christ have different functions**, "For just as each of us has one body with many members, and these members do not all have the same function, so in Christ we, though many, form one body, and each member belongs to all the others." (Rom 12:4-5).

- **Every member's ministry causes the body to grow**, "From him the whole body, joined and held together by every supporting ligament, grows and builds itself up in love, as each part does its work." (Eph 4:16)

✐ Assignment
What is implied in the Scripture calling the church 'the Body of Christ'?

The church as a building

In the Old Testament both the Tabernacle and Temple were of great importance in terms of the worship of God. God had chosen to come and dwell in his house among his people. In the New Testament the plan of God was brought even closer. The people of God were called to be a house for God to dwell in, by the Spirit, "And in him you too are being built together to become a dwelling in which God lives by his Spirit." (Eph 2:21-22). Peter uses the same analogy when he says of believers, "you also, like living stones, are being built into a spiritual house" (1 Pet 2:5).

- **Christ is the foundation to be built on**, "For no one can lay any foundation other than the one already laid, which is Jesus Christ." (1 Cor 3:11)

- **Christ is the cornerstone to build on**, "For in Scripture it says: "See, I lay a stone in Zion, a chosen and precious cornerstone" (1 Pet 2:6).

- **Christ is the head or Capstone of the building**, "The stone the builders rejected has become the cornerstone [capstone]." (1 Pet 2:7).

The church as a family

The image of the family runs through all the Bible teaching on the church. The corporate identity of the family comes from God as Father, "For this reason I kneel before the Father, from whom every family in heaven and on earth derives its name." (Eph 3:14-15). Fellow members of the church are identified as brothers and sisters and older ones as fathers and mothers, "Do not rebuke an older man harshly, but exhort him as if he were your father. Treat younger men as brothers, older women as mothers, and younger women as sisters, with absolute purity." (1 Tim 5:1-2). Paul commends the church for loving the family of God, "And in fact, you do love all of God's family throughout Macedonia. (1 The 4:10). Leaders are to function as spiritual fathers in the faith "Even if you had ten thousand guardians in Christ, you do not have many fathers, for in Christ Jesus I became your father through the gospel." (1 Cor 4:15).

The church as a bride

The analogy of the bride brings out the love relationship between Christ and his people. It is using the closest human relationship on earth to indicate the intimacy of that union with Christ.

- **Christ is the heavenly bridegroom**, "How can the guests of the bridegroom mourn while he is with them?" (Mat 9:15); (see also the parable of the ten virgins, Mat 25:1-13).
- **The church is engaged to be married to Christ**, "I am jealous for you with a godly jealousy. I promised you to one husband, to Christ, so that I might present you as a pure virgin to him." (2 Cor 11:2).
- **The church must be ready for her husband**, "For the wedding of the Lamb has come, and his bride has made herself ready." (Rev 19:7).
- **Christ loves the church as his wife**, "Husbands, love your wives, just as Christ loved the church and gave himself up for her" (Eph 5:25).

The church as the ground & pillar of truth

Paul describes believers as that "God's household, which is the church of the living God, the pillar and foundation of the truth." (1 Tim 3:15). This shows the high calling and responsibility of the church in this world. Believers have been called by Christ to be the light of the world. That light is the knowledge of the truth with which the church has been entrusted - it is the keys to the kingdom of God. No other company of people have been entrusted with such a body of truth. That knowledge is far more important than all the scientific and cultural knowledge built up by the learning faculties of the world. The church has been grounded on truth, and is built up as a citadel of truth. With regard to this analogy of the church, individuals are recognised as pillars in the church, "James, Cephas and John, those esteemed as pillars," (Gal 2:9). Christ promised that over-comers would be pillars in the temple of God, "The one who is victorious I will make a pillar in the temple of my God." (Rev 3:12).

The unity of the church

The great purpose of Christ coming into the world was to "seek and to save that which was lost", and then to bring those redeemed people into a deep sense of oneness. Jesus said, "and there shall be one flock and one shepherd" (Jhn 10:16).

In his great high priestly prayer Jesus prayed for all who would believe on his name, "that all of them may be one, Father, just as you are in me and I am in you. May they also be in us so that the world may believe that you have sent me." (Jhn 17:21).

This unity of believers, throughout the world, does not require a huge system of church government to unite it. The church may be divided into groupings and denominations, but a unity of heart and co-operation between the different groups should still exist. With all its diverse structures the whole Church is called to live under the headship of Christ. The common declaration of the true church everywhere is, "There is one body and one Spirit, just as you were called to one hope when you were called; one Lord, one faith, one baptism; one God and Father of all" (Eph 4:5-6).

Worship and ministry in the church

The New Testament church was a community of believers committed to Jesus Christ and to each other. They met regularly to encourage one another in faith and love, and to unite in the praise and worship of God. The church existed for the praise and worship of God, "in order that we, who were the first to put our hope in Christ, might be for the praise of his glory." (Eph 1:12). The basic elements in their meeting together are given to us in (Act 2:42),

1. Apostolic teaching
2. Fellowship
3. Breaking bread
4. Prayers.

From the little that we know of the customs of the early church it is clear that most did not meet in any special building. The first believers used the temple as a meeting place, because they were Jews living in Jerusalem, (Act 2:46, 3:1). However, this was short lived because of the rift that came between the Judaisers and Christians. It was soon apparent that the old wine-skins could not contain the new wine of the gospel. The believers met in small house groups, and in larger congregations.

In those times of public worship everyone was expected to bring a helpful ministry to the group. Paul exhorted the Corinthians, "When you come together, each of you has a hymn, or a word of instruction, a revelation, a tongue or an interpretation. Everything must be done so that the church may be built up." (1 Cor 14:26). To the Ephesians he wrote, "speaking to one another with psalms, hymns, and songs from the Spirit. Sing and make music from your heart to the Lord," (Eph 5:19). It was at such times that the gifts of the Spirit were manifested for the benefit of all (1 Cor 12 & 14). Emphasis was placed on the reading and exposition of scripture, and the singing of both Old Testament Psalms and new hymns of praise to Christ, "Let the message of Christ dwell among you richly as you teach and admonish one another with all wisdom through psalms, hymns, and songs from the Spirit, singing to God with gratitude in your hearts." (Col 3:16-17).

It is quite probable that the Doxologies used by Paul, in his epistles, were also used throughout the church as part of worship to God. He exclaimed, "Oh, the depth of the riches of the wisdom and knowledge of God! How unsearchable his judgements, and his paths beyond tracing out! "Who has known the mind of the Lord? Or who has been his counsellor?" "Who has ever given to God, that God should repay them?" For from him and through him and for him are all things. To him be the glory forever! Amen." (Rom 11:33-36). And again, "Now to him who is able to do immeasurably more than all we ask or imagine, according to his power that is at work within us, to him be glory in the church and in Christ Jesus throughout all generations, for ever and ever! Amen." (Eph 3:20-21, see also 1 Tim 2:3-6).

✎ Assignment
In which ways can the people of God be used in ministry in the church?

The government of the church

The New Testament does not lay down a strict form of ecclesiastical government, such as we have in many denominations today. However, it does show that some form of structure was quickly laid down for the protection, feeding and growth of the church. That same structure, along with the same ministry and offices, should be in the church today. In that sense, the New Testament lays down a pattern for every generation to follow.

It is clear that the pioneering apostles held a position of great influence in the churches they founded. The book of Act show the twelve apostles were organising, teaching etc. in Jerusalem and Judea.

The people who believed the preaching of the apostles committed themselves to it with diligence, "They devoted themselves to the apostles' teaching and to fellowship, to the breaking of bread and to prayer." (Act 2:42).

The main task of the apostles was the teaching of the Scriptures, "So the Twelve gathered all the disciples together and said, 'It would not be right for us to neglect the ministry of the word of God in order to wait on tables'." (Act 6:2).

Men of prophetic calling worked closely together with the apostles, "During this time some prophets came down from Jerusalem to Antioch." (Act 11:27). Those prophets brought words of exhortation regarding the purpose of the Church, in terms of the new covenant, "Judas and Silas, who themselves were prophets, said much to encourage and strengthen the believers" (Act 15:32). There were other itinerant men who pioneered as evangelists. They proclaimed the word of the gospel in new territory with great power, "Philip went down to a city in Samaria and proclaimed the Messiah there." (Act 8:5-6).

The apostles ordained elders in every church to care for the local church, "Paul and Barnabas appointed elders for them in each church and, with prayer and fasting, committed them to the Lord, in whom they had put their trust." (Act 14:23). The elders, men of good character, were to protect the people from false teachers and nurture them in the word of God, "Keep watch over yourselves and all the flock of which the Holy Spirit has made you overseers. Be shepherds of the church of God, which he bought with his own blood." (Act 20:28). Those men carried the responsibility for the life and direction of the local church.

Every local church had its own leadership, and this meant that a degree of autonomy was exercised by each church. However, the idea of totally independent churches was foreign to the New Testament Church. There was an interdependence expressed between churches. This was shown in the way they shared the teaching letters sent by the apostle, "After this letter has been read to you, see that it is also read in the church of the Laodiceans and that you in turn read the letter from Laodicea." (Col 4:16). It was also expressed in the sending of financial aid from one church to another, "The disciples, as each one was able, decided to provide help for the brothers and sisters living in Judea." (Act 11:29). Also, constant links were kept with the churches by the pioneering apostles, with Paul sending younger apostles to visit the various centres (2 Cor 8:16-18 cp. Eph 6:21-22).

Purpose of the church in this present age

The church through the centuries has been composed of people who have been "born again" by God's Spirit. They were indwelt, and empowered by the Holy Spirit. These people were brought together into local churches, united in their love of Christ and their care for each other. They were a people who "tasted of the power of the age to come" and yet lived in this "present age". The Church was called to be a powerful witness of the great wisdom of God, to principalities, "His intent was that now, through the church, the manifold wisdom of God should be made known to the rulers and authorities in the heavenly realms," (Eph 3:10). The Church was also prepared by God to become a living witness to the reality of His Son, Jesus Christ, in the world.

The great commission given to this people was to carry the gospel of the Kingdom of God, and disciple all nations. They were to proclaim the truth regarding Jesus Christ as the Son of God, who is Lord of all. They were called to make known the power and value of his atoning death, and the triumph of his resurrection.

They carried a message to all people, "I have declared to both Jews and Greeks that they must turn to God in repentance and have faith in our Lord Jesus." (Act 20:21). Christ promised his continual presence in the church for this work to be accomplished, "And surely I am with you always, to the very end of the age." (Mat 28:19-20). This promise was fulfilled by the outpouring of the Spirit, who was given to empower believers to be witnesses of Christ in the world, "But you will receive power when the Holy Spirit comes on you; and you will be my witnesses in Jerusalem, and in all Judea and Samaria, and to the ends of the earth." (Act 1:8). With the enabling power of the Spirit they carried the gospel from the 'upper room', (Act 1:13), into every 'living room' in the city, "'We gave you strict orders not to teach in this name,' he said. 'Yet you have filled Jerusalem with your teaching'" (Act 5:28).

Assignment
What is the main purpose of the church in the world today?

Conclusion

There may be many details we are not given with regard to the life, ministry and government of the early church. However, enough is revealed for us to know that the church was called to be a community of believers in a living relationship with Jesus Christ. They were called to share and reveal his very life and ministry on earth. In that relationship they acknowledged, worshipped and proclaimed the name of the triune God of heaven and earth. They were bound to each other in love and faith, and ministered to each others needs. Under the grace of God, and by the empowering of the Spirit, they were called to reveal the love of God to the world. As witnesses of Christ they were to proclaim the gospel of the Kingdom to the ends of the earth. To accomplish these ends, the people of God were placed into local settings under wise and caring leaders. The work of those leaders was to nurture and develop the saints so that they too could be released into works of ministry.

Notes

God's Eternal Purpose

Study 9

The Doctrine of Angels & Demons

📖 **Revelation 5:8-14**

Introduction

Over the years there has been little serious attention given to the subject of angels and demons. Consequently, many Christians do not see the importance of the issues. On the one hand, the Bible presents a fascinating account of the order and activity of holy, powerful beings that are utterly committed to working out God's will. On the other hand, we are introduced to dark beings that are utterly opposed to God and his people.

The nature and order of angels

The word 'angel' means messenger, which gives us an immediate insight into their main function with regard to mankind. In their origin they were all bright, glorious and powerful creatures. They have not existed from eternity but are created beings that God brought into existence before the world began. Though they are powerful beings they are all under God's command, he is the 'Lord of hosts' (angels).

> *We are clearly told that angels are all inferior in power and glory to the Son of God.*

The Bible clearly shows us that angels are all inferior in power and glory to the Son of God, "For to which of the angels did God ever say, 'You are my Son; today I have become your Father'?" (Heb 1:5-6). Angels were in fact created by the Son, "For in him all things were created: things in heaven and on earth," (Col 1:16). At present they are superior in power and majesty to man, "What is mankind that you are mindful of them, a son of man that you care for him? You made them a little lower than the angels;" (Heb 2:6-7).

They are spoken of as spirits, "He makes winds (spirits) his messengers," (Psa 104:4). They do not have physical bodies as we have, but they do have spiritual bodies and can appear in human form, "Abraham looked up and saw three men standing nearby." (Gen 18:2) which leads

God's Eternal Purpose: An introduction to Christian doctrine

on to, "The two angels arrived at Sodom" (Gen 19:1).

It is noted that probably all angels in the Bible are referred to as 'he' which suggests that they are at least male in appearance (but look at Zec 5:9). However, they are not divided into male and female in the way that mankind is, in our present state, "At the resurrection people will neither marry nor be given in marriage; they will be like the angels in heaven." (Mat 22:30). It seems also that angels do not die as we do, "and they can no longer die; for they are like the angels." (Luk 20:36). The writer of Hebrews says our Lord was made "lower than the angels" (Heb 2:9), for the purpose of entering death. This indicates that, apart from taking such a position, Christ could not have died.

The various ranks among angels

In several scriptures we are introduced to various orders of holy beings, "far above all rule and authority, power and dominion, and every name that is invoked," (Eph 1:21). We are also introduced to an order of dark beings, "For our struggle is not against flesh and blood, but against the rulers, against the authorities, against the powers of this dark world and against the spiritual forces of evil in the heavenly realms." (Eph 6:12). It appears that there is an ascending order of power among these beings, some of which are good and some evil.

Some angels are called 'holy angels' (Luk 9:26), some are called 'elect angels' (1 Tim 5:21) and some are called 'ministering spirits' (Heb 1:14). Among these are creatures called 'cherubim', "The LORD reigns ... he sits enthroned between the cherubim," (Psa 99:1, cp. Eze 10:3). Others are called 'seraphim' (fiery), "I saw the Lord ... seated on a throne ... Above him were seraphim, each with six wings:" (Isa 6:1-2). In the book of Revelation we are introduced to mysterious beings called "living creatures" (Rev 4:6). We know very little about any of these beings, but every mention of them in the scripture puts them in some exalted position in the manifest glory of God. There is an archangel mentioned, who is linked with the second coming of Christ, "For the Lord himself will come down from heaven, with a loud command, with the voice of the archangel and with the trumpet call of God" (1 The 4:16). In Jud we are told of Michael the archangel who contended with Satan over the body of Moses (Jud 1:9). This mighty angel has had a peculiar responsibility for the nation of Israel, "Then Michael, one of the chief princes, came to help me," (Dan 10:13).

The number of angels

How many angels are there? The answer is countless numbers. The Lord in Gethsemane said he could call for twelve legions of angels to defend him, (Mat 26:53), - a legion contained between 3000 and 6000 troops. The shepherds at the birth of Christ saw, "a great company of the heavenly host," (Luk 2:13). In Revelations John saw a myriad angels, "numbering thousands upon thousands, and ten thousand times ten thousand." (Rev 5:11).

These 'creatures' are depicted as being far more powerful and glorious than we are in our present state. What the future state of the redeemed will be is less obvious, "It is not to angels that he has subjected the world to come," (Heb 2:5-11). The future position of redeemed mankind may be more glorious than angels.

The role of the Holy angels in worship

The natural habitation of the holy angels is 'heaven', in the manifest presence of God. In that privileged and exalted place, their major occupation is to worship God and his Christ, and to do his will, "In a loud voice they were saying: 'Worthy is the Lamb, who was slain, to receive power and wealth and wisdom and strength and honour and glory and praise'!" (Rev 5:11-12). Jesus gives us a glimpse of the position and activity of angels as they watch over children, "For I tell you that their angels in heaven always see the face of my Father in heaven." (Mat 18:10). They constantly attend on God and watch for any indication of his will for them.

The ministry of angels to Christ

It is worth noting the significant role that angels played in the life of our Lord Jesus when he was on earth.

There was extensive angelic activity around the birth of Christ.
An angel appeared to Zacharius, (Luk 1:11-12); to Mary, (Luk 1:26-27); to Joseph, (Mat 1:20); and the shepherds, (Luk 2:9,13).

Angels came to minister help to Christ during his ministry.
After the period of temptation, "Then the devil left him, and angels came and attended him." (Mat 4:11). They came to him again in the garden of Gethsemane, "An angel from heaven appeared to him and strengthened him." (Luk 22:43).

They were also very active at the resurrection.
The announcement of the resurrection, (Mat 28:2, Mar 16:5).
At the ascension, (Acts 1:10-11).

The ministry of angels to believers

Angelic beings have played a significant role in working out God's purposes for redeemed humanity. "Are not all angels ministering spirits sent to serve those who will inherit salvation?" (Heb 1:14)

In this role they seem to be fascinated with the theme of salvation and try to understand the mystery of God's grace and forgiveness, "Even angels long to look into these things." (1 Pet 1:12). It seems that in their own order they have no revelation of the grace of God. We never read of any angel experiencing the forgiveness of God.

Angels were used to reveal God's purposes to men, such as:

- **Abraham** was shown that God would destroy Sodom and Gomorrah, (Gen 18).
- **Gideon** was visited by the angel of the Lord and told of God's purpose for his life, (Jdg 6:11-12).
- **Zacharias** was told of the importance of the son he would have, (Luk 1:11-17).
- **Cornelius** had an angel sent to him, with the instruction to send for Peter who would show him the way of salvation. It should be noted, that the angel did not attempt to

bring the gospel to Cornelius, but told him to call for Peter, (Act 10).

These beings were also sent to protect God's people in time of danger "For he will command his angels concerning you to guard you in all your ways;" (Psa 91:11). They also brought comfort and cheer to Paul in the shipwreck "Last night an angel of the God to whom I belong and whom I serve stood beside me" (Acts 27:22-24). One of the very precious things they have been involved in, is the transporting of God's people into Paradise when they die, "The time came when the beggar died and the angels carried him to Abraham's side." (Luk 16:22). They have also been used to strike at the enemies of God's people, as in the case of Herod, "because Herod did not give praise to God, an angel of the Lord struck him down, and he was eaten by worms and died." (Act 12:23).

The role of angels at the end of the Age

With regard to God's people, the final work that angels are given is in the last day, at the return of Christ. The angels will be used to gather together God's elect from all the earth, "And he will send his angels with a loud trumpet call, and they will gather his elect from the four winds, from one end of the heavens to the other." (Mat 24:31). When interpreting the parable of the good and bad seed Jesus says, "The Son of Man will send out his angels, and they will weed out of his kingdom everything that causes sin and all who do evil. They will throw them into the blazing furnace," (Mat 13:41-42).

✎ Assignment
What does the Scripture teach us about the ministry of angels in the lives of believers?

The Devil and the fallen angels

What does the Bible say about those spirit beings that are opposed to God and his people? Understanding their nature and activities will help us to understand why the world keeps going wrong, and why we as believers sometimes struggle with life.

"It is quite impossible to understand human history without considering what the Bible tells us about these fallen or evil angels. We cannot hope to understand man as he is today, we cannot hope to understand the world, apart from this. And it increasingly seems to me that the essence of the error which most people seem to make, even in the history of the twentieth century to which we belong, is that they fail to consider the biblical doctrine of the devil and his angels".

- Lloyd-Jones 'Great Doctrine Series - Vol. 1' p.115

The names of the Devil

The account of the Devil and his opposition to God runs right through the Bible from Genesis to Revelation. If we look at the descriptions and names that the Bible gives to this creature it will enlighten us as to his essential nature and character:-

- **Satan** *[adversary]* - "I am sending you to them to open their eyes and turn them from darkness to light, and from the power of Satan to God" (Acts 26:18).

- **The prince or ruler of this world** – "Now is the time for judgement on this world; now the prince of this world will be driven out." (Jhn 12:31, see also Jhn 14:30, Jhn 16:11).

- **Devil** [*slanderer*] – "so that he will not fall into disgrace and into the devil's trap." (1 Tim 3:7, see also Mat 4:1).

- **The god of this age** – "The god of this age has blinded the minds of unbelievers," (2 Cor 4:4).

- **Beelzebul** [*lord of flies*] – The Scribes said, "He is possessed by Beelzebul! By the prince of demons he is driving out demons." (Mar 3:22).

- **The ruler of the power of the air** – "when you followed the ways of this world and of the ruler of the kingdom of the air," (Eph 2:2).

- **Lucifer** [*morning star or brightness*] – "How you have fallen from heaven, morning star, son of the dawn" (Isa 14:12).

- **The dragon** – "He seized the dragon, that ancient serpent, who is the devil," (Rev 20:2).

- **The serpent** – "But I am afraid that just as Eve was deceived by the serpent's cunning, your minds may somehow be led astray" (2 Cor 11:3).

- **The wicked one** – "I am writing to you, young men, because you have overcome the evil one." (1 Jhn 2:13, see also 1 Jhn 5:18).

- **The angel of the bottomless pit** – "They had as king over them the angel of the Abyss," (Rev 9:11)

- **Abaddon** or **Apollyon** [*destroying angel*] – "whose name in Hebrew is Abaddon and in Greek is Apollyon." (Rev 9:11).

- **A roaring lion** – "Your enemy the devil prowls around like a roaring lion looking for someone to devour." (1 Pet 5:8).

- **The evil one** – "My prayer is not that you take them out of the world but that you protect them from the evil one." (Jhn 17:15, see also Mat 13:19).

- **The tempter** – "I was afraid that in some way the tempter had tempted you and that our labours might have been in vain." (1 The 3:5).

- **The enemy** – "and the enemy who sows them is the devil." (Mat 13:39)

- **Belial** [*worthless one*] – "What harmony is there between Christ and Belial?" (2 Cor 6:15).

A personal being

The Devil is not just an evil force, but is a personal being. This is shown in the personal encounters that the Lord experienced in the wilderness temptations. Some Christians put all temptation down to a lack in themselves. Sometimes temptation comes because of that, but at other times it is a direct assault of the Devil. It was an evil, personal being that sought permission from God to afflict Job, (Job 1:6-12). The same can be said of the lesser beings, called demons or evil spirits, who are under the authority of Satan. The Devil stands at the head of an organised kingdom of lesser spirits, who are all actively opposed to God and his plan of redemption. "The great dragon was hurled down--that ancient serpent called the devil, or Satan, who leads the whole world astray. He was hurled to the earth, and his angels with him." (Rev 12:9).

The origin of the Devil

From where does this evil creature come? The Bible does not say a lot about these things, but Ezekiel speaks of the catastrophic fall of some exalted being who may well be Satan himself (Eze 28:11-19). This passage speaks of the king of Tyre but then speaks of a far greater being who had an exalted position before God, "You were the seal of perfection, full of wisdom and perfect in beauty. You were in Eden, the garden of God;" (v.12). He is described as the anointed cherub, "You were anointed as a guardian cherub (*outspread*)," (v.14). This being was the highest of all the created spirits. He may have been intended to take a leading role in the created universe, to represent the worship and adoration of God. We learn that he was created perfect, "till wickedness was found in you." (v.15). At that point he became consumed with pride and sought to exalt himself above God.

Isaiah also speaks prophetically about some exalted being who may well be identified with Satan,

"How you have fallen from heaven, morning star, son of the dawn! ... you who once laid low the nations! You said in your heart, 'I will ascend to the heavens; I will raise my throne above the stars of God; ... I will make myself like the Most High'." (Isa 14:12-15).

This cherub, who was created glorious, became a terrifying creature, utterly opposed to God. We should not dismiss all these creatures as if they had no authority. In Jud we learn how the archangel Michael would not foolishly revile the Devil but said, "The Lord rebuke you" (Jud 1:9).

The mystery of all this is that God allows the Devil to continue to hold a position of power, and to do certain evil things. However, it must be remembered that, at all times, he is under the control of God and cannot go further than God allows.

The work of the Devil on unbelievers

The works of the Devil are controlled by his character. He is called a deceiver, a liar, a slanderer and Jesus calls him a thief and a murderer (Jhn 8:44). After his fall from heaven, his first major objective was to bring about the fall of man. He succeeded in tempting Adam and Eve and set them in opposition to the rule of God. This resulted in the whole human race being brought into a coalition with him, and against God. Paul gives us an insight into the influence that the Devil has upon mankind in this coalition "in which you used to live when you followed the ways of this world and of the ruler of the kingdom of the air, the spirit who is now at work in those who are disobedient." (Eph 2:2). Jesus was referring to the relationship between mankind and the Devil when he spoke to the Pharisees,"You belong to your father, the devil," (Jhn 8:44). In his first letter, John shows the different state of believers and unbelievers "We know that we are children of God, and that the whole world is under the control of the evil one"

(1 Jhn 5:19). The devil has been successful because he holds people in darkness,"The god of this age has blinded the minds of unbelievers, so that they cannot see the light of the gospel that displays the glory of Christ, who is the image of God." (2 Cor 4:3,4). Jesus also tells us that, 'the wicked one' snatches away the seed of the Kingdom from the heart of those who do not understand, (Mat 13:19,39). Satan will come and deceive many by lying wonders, "The coming of the lawless one will be in accordance with how Satan works. He will use all sorts of displays of power through signs and wonders that serve the lie," (2 The 2:9).

✏ Assignment
In which ways does Satan try to stop people becoming Christians?

The work of the Devil on believers

The Devil is vicious, and seeks to frustrate those who have submitted themselves to Christ and the rule of God. He is called the accuser of the brethren, "For the accuser of our brothers and sisters, who accuses them before our God day and night, has been hurled down." (Rev 12:10). An example of such accusation is given in Zechariah, "Then he showed me Joshua the high priest standing before the angel of the LORD, and Satan standing at his right side to accuse him." (Zec 3:1-2). He seeks to hinder the servants of God in their work of promoting the Gospel, "For we wanted to come to you--certainly I, Paul, did, again and again--but Satan blocked our way." (1 The 2:18). Even though God allowed this 'hindering' he brought good out of it. Paul could not go back to the city of Thessalonica, but he sent letters to the saints there. A record of these letters have been preserved for us, and the church has benefited from them ever since.

The devil shoots his fiery darts at the saints, "take up the shield of faith, with which you can extinguish all the flaming arrows of the evil one" (Eph 6:16). Jesus said to Peter, "Simon, Simon, Satan has asked to sift all of you as wheat." (Luk 22:31) but the prayer of Christ prevailed for him, though not without some serious failure. Satan stirred up greed in Ananias and Sapphira, "Ananias, how is it that Satan has so filled your heart that you have lied to the Holy Spirit" (Acts 5:3).

He finds ways of afflicting the bodies of God's people "I was given a thorn in my flesh, a messenger of Satan, to torment me." (2 Cor 12:7). The woman who was healed by Jesus after 18 years of affliction, was said to have been bound by Satan, "Then should not this woman, a daughter of Abraham, whom Satan has kept bound for eighteen long years, be set free on the Sabbath day from what bound her?" (Luk 13:16).

He sometimes disguises himself as an 'angel of light' in order to delude God's people, and bring evil influence to the church, "And no wonder, for Satan himself masquerades as an angel of light." (2 Cor 11:14). The devil can make offers of power and glory in this world to deviate believers from the way of the cross, "I will give you all their authority and splendour; it has been given to me, and I can give it to anyone I want to." (Luk 4:6). He seeks to take advantage of situations in the church, "in order that Satan might not outwit us. For we are not unaware of his schemes." (2 Cor 2:11). He tries to use occasions in married life to tempt believers, "Do not deprive each other except perhaps by mutual consent and for a time, ... Then come together again so that Satan will not tempt you because of your lack of self-control." (1 Cor 7:5).

Satan tries to turn our minds to concentrate on what pleases man rather than God, "Get behind me, Satan! You are a stumbling block to me; you do not have in mind the concerns of

God, but merely human concerns." (Mat 16:23). He seeks to deceive believers, to turn them from the truth, to a false Jesus, a false spirit and a false gospel, "But I am afraid that just as Eve was deceived by the serpent's cunning, your minds may somehow be led astray from your sincere and pure devotion to Christ. For if someone comes to you and **preaches a Jesus other** than the Jesus we preached, or if you receive a **different spirit** from the Spirit you received, or a **different gospel** from the one you accepted," (2 Cor 11:3-4).

Assignment
What should believers do to combat the schemes of the devil?

God's actions against the Devil

God has already taken action against the Devil and his angels. Jesus said, "I saw Satan fall like lightning from heaven." (Luk 10:18, see also Rev 12:7-9). Peter tells us how God dealt with some of the angels that sinned, "For if God did not spare angels when they sinned, but sent them to hell (tartarus), putting them in chains of darkness to be held for judgement;" (2 Pet 2:4, see also Jud 1:6). We must always remember that the Devil and his hoards are limited in power, and always come under the rule of God. It is said of Christ, "The reason the Son of God appeared was to destroy the devil's work." (1 Jhn 3:8). Through his sinless life, his atoning death and resurrection, Christ has already overcome the Devil, "Now is the time for judgement on this world; now the prince of this world will be driven out." (Jhn 12:31).

Christ brought about this triumph over Satan, not only for himself, but on the behalf of all who believe on him. Because of this believers have been given authority to resist Satan. In Scripture we are called to submit to God then, "Resist the devil, and he will flee from you." (Jam 4:7). John reminds us in Revelation that the saints, "triumphed over him by the blood of the Lamb and by the word of their testimony;" (Rev 12:11). Paul calls us to put on the whole armour of God, "Put on the full armour of God, so that you can take your stand against the devil's schemes (*methodeia*)." (Eph 6:11). It is the Devil's wicked schemes we are to fight, rather than his might. John shows us the great possibilities for believers, in their salvation through Christ, "We know that anyone born of God does not continue to sin; the One who was born of God keeps them safe, and the evil one cannot harm them." (1 Jhn 5:18). We must remember that whatever power God allows Satan to have, it is always under Gods control.

We should remind the Devil that his end is unalterably settled, by the decree of God, "And the devil, who deceived them, was thrown into the lake of burning sulphur ... They will be tormented day and night for ever and ever." (Rev 20:10).

Notes

God's Eternal Purpose

Study 10
The Doctrine of the Last Things

📖 **1 Thessalonians 4:13-18 & 5:1-11**

Introduction

The theme of the end times and the second coming of Christ are given a prominent place in the New Testament. It is referred to over three hundred times, and whole chapters are devoted to it. The Lord's coming is set before us as the great hope of the church, when our salvation will come to its fullness.

There are two parts of the Bible that Christians have often disagreed over. The first is the Old Testament prophetic Scriptures, especially the parts that have not yet been fulfilled. The second is the New Testament Scriptures dealing with events that will take place when Christ returns to this world, to complete salvation.

The certainty of Christ's return

Whilst there is disagreement among Christians over the sequence of events of the last times, there is definite agreement over the fact that Christ will return, as a glorified man, to the earth.

- **Jesus told his disciples that he would return for them**, "I will come back and take you to be with me that you also may be where I am." (Jhn 14:3, cp. Mat 24:44).

- **Angels declared Christ's return to the disciples**, "This same Jesus, who has been taken from you into heaven, will come back in the same way you have seen him go into heaven." (Act 1:11).

- **The apostles taught the return of Christ**, "and to wait for his Son from heaven ... Jesus, who rescues us from the coming wrath." (1 The 1:10, see also 1 John 3:2). It was clearly taught by the writer of Hebrews, "he will appear a second time, not to bear sin, but to bring salvation to those who are waiting for him." (Heb 9:28).

The one thing we do not know about the return of Christ is the exact time he will come, "But about that day or hour no one knows, not even the angels in heaven, nor the Son, but only the Father" (Mar 13:32, see also Mat 24:36). Many individuals, and groups have attempted to work out the specific date of Christ's Coming, but time has shown them to have made foolish predictions. Christ expects believers to live in the expectation of his return by being actively involved in his Kingdom business. "It's like a man going away: He leaves his house and puts his servants in charge, ... and tells the one at the door to keep watch. Therefore keep watch because you do not know when the owner of the house will come back--whether in the evening, or at midnight, or when the rooster crows, or at dawn. If he comes suddenly, do not let him find you sleeping. What I say to you, I say to everyone: Watch!" (Mar 13:34-37).

Four views of the Second Coming of Christ

Pre-Millennial view

This view of the Coming of Christ is often associated with a system of Bible teaching, known as 'Dispensationalism'. In this system men tried to interpret Bible history as a series of seven dispensations. They taught that God dealt with mankind in a distinct way during each period of time. This is a very inadequate approach to Scripture, which does not clearly describe God's dealings with mankind through the ages. The dispensations outlined in this view are:

1. Innocence - Adam and Eve
2. Conscience - Early civilisation
3. Human Government - After the flood
4. Promise - Abraham onwards
5. Law - Moses
6. Grace - Christ and church age
7. Kingdom - Return of Christ

This teaching became very popular from the 1820s onward. It presented a rather pessimistic view of the church in the end times. It was taken up by J. N. Darby, who taught that the second coming of Christ was in two phases.

The first phase, was in Christ 'coming to the air' when there was to be a 'secret rapture' of believers to heaven. This coming of Christ, was sometimes seen as a rescue mission, that would bring the church age to an end. It would lead into a seven year period of 'tribulation' upon the earth, with the 'man of lawlessness' having great power among the nations.

The second phase would occur when Christ came in glory with his saints, to set up his Millennial kingdom on earth. The restored nation of Israel would be at the centre of this kingdom. At the end of the thousand years, Satan was to be loosed from the deep pit. Satan would stir up rebellion against Christ, but Christ would overcome and destroy his enemies. This would be followed by the resurrection of unbelievers and the final judgement. The end for Satan, and all of humanity that would not accept the gospel of Christ, was the 'lake of fire'. The new heavens and new earth would be inhabited by Christ and his people.

Pre-Millennial view timeline

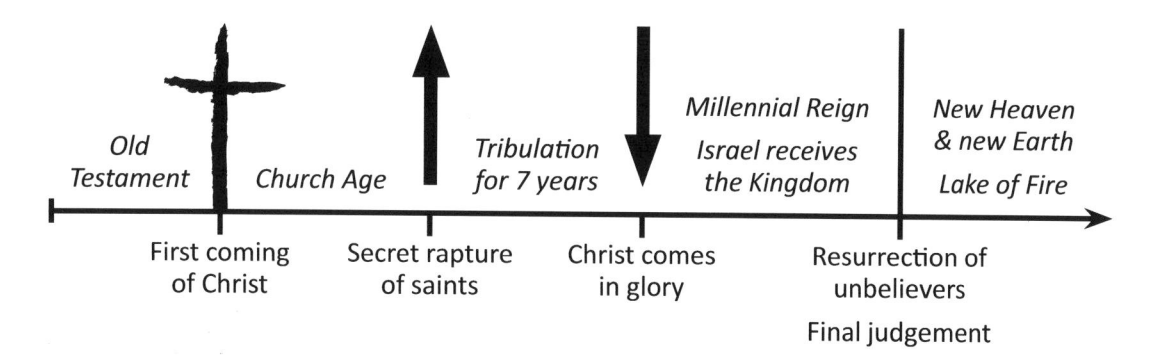

Timeline shows: Old Testament | First coming of Christ (cross) | Church Age | Secret rapture of saints (up arrow) | Tribulation for 7 years | Christ comes in glory (down arrow) | Millennial Reign, Israel receives the Kingdom | Resurrection of unbelievers, Final judgement | New Heaven & new Earth, Lake of Fire

A-Millennial view

The early teachers of this view, such as Augustine, saw the millennium of Revelation 20 as symbolic of a period of time, from the resurrection of Christ to his 'parousia' (appearing). This was identified as the 'church age', or the 'age of the gospel', in which Satan was bound through the redemptive, victorious work of Christ. The Protestant Reformers of the 16th century modified this view, and saw the millennium as a thousand year reign of the gospel, from Christ into the Middle Ages. This Millennium of progress was followed by the release of Satan (Rev 20:7). They saw the rise of the papacy as the work of Satan. As leaders of the emerging new churches they saw themselves restoring the true gospel, and they expected the imminent return of Christ. At Christ's coming there was to be the general resurrection of all peoples. This would be followed by the final judgement, and the eternal state settled for both believers and unbelievers.

A-Millennial view timeline

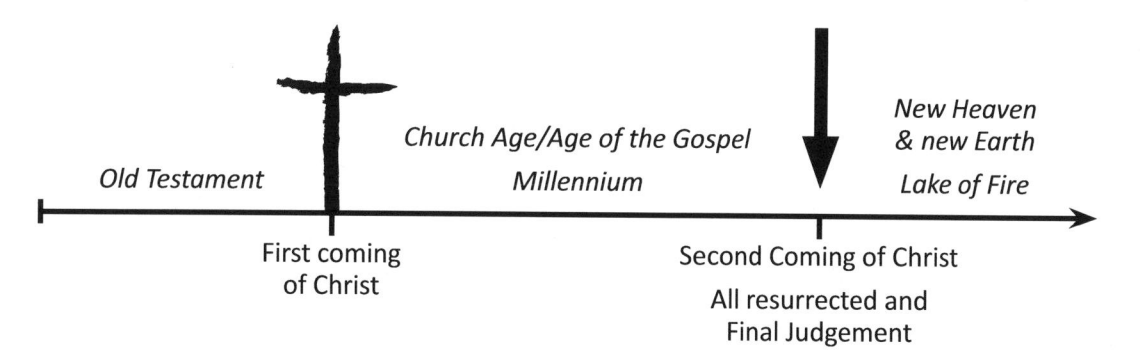

Timeline shows: Old Testament | First coming of Christ (cross) | Church Age/Age of the Gospel, Millennium | Second Coming of Christ, All resurrected and Final Judgement (down arrow) | New Heaven & new Earth, Lake of Fire

Post-Millennial view

Some Reformers of the 16th century took a different view of the millennium. They were more hopeful about the emerging churches under Protestant leadership. Some viewed the 'thousand years' as a literal time line, when the reign of Christ would be displayed through the Church and the gospel would flourish over all the world. Others saw it as a symbolic, undefined time until the coming of Christ. Both groups held an over optimistic view of the Church and the end times. Their view of the resurrection and final state was in line with the A-millennialist view.

God's Eternal Purpose: An introduction to Christian doctrine

Post-Millennial view timeline

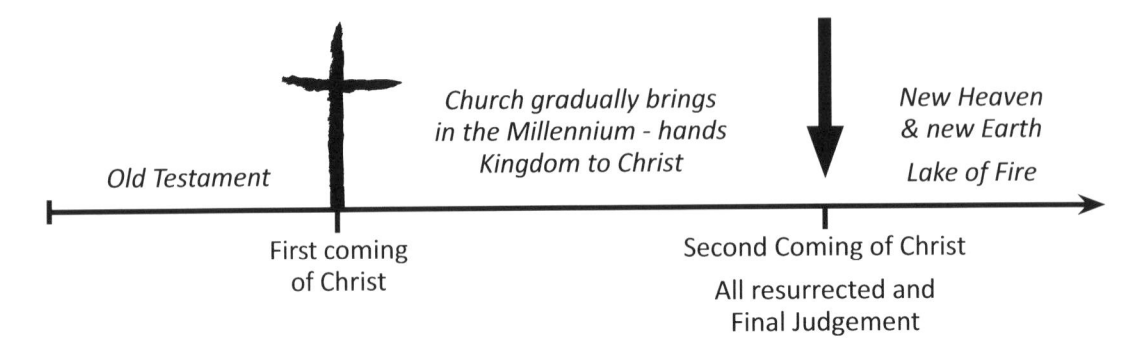

```
Old Testament | Church gradually brings    | New Heaven
              | in the Millennium - hands  | & new Earth
              | Kingdom to Christ          | Lake of Fire
──────────────┼────────────────────────────┼──────────────→
      First coming              Second Coming of Christ
       of Christ                 All resurrected and
                                  Final Judgement
```

Older Pre-Millennial view

A more balanced view was presented by some of the early church fathers. This was representative of both the Church-age and the end times, and embraced a belief in the pre-Millennial return of Christ, Some of the more well known of the early fathers holding this view were, Papias (AD 60-130), Justin (AD 100-165), Irenaeus (AD 130-200) and Tertullian (AD 160-225). They expected the coming of Christ in glory to bring about the resurrection of believers and a millennial reign of Christ over the earth. This was to be an idyllic age, a restored paradise, on a renewed earth. There would be peace among the animals and great fruitfulness in the earth. After this time would come the resurrection of unbelievers, the final judgement and the eternal state.

Older Pre-Millennial view timeline

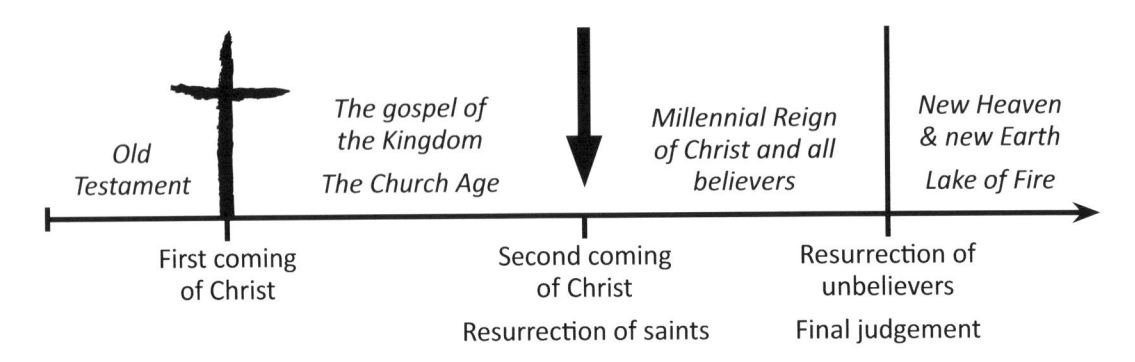

```
Old        | The gospel of   | Millennial Reign | New Heaven
Testament  | the Kingdom     | of Christ and all| & new Earth
           | The Church Age  | believers        | Lake of Fire
───────────┼─────────────────┼──────────────────┼──────────────→
  First coming        Second coming      Resurrection of
   of Christ           of Christ          unbelievers
                    Resurrection of saints  Final judgement
```

The incentive of the coming of Christ

The teaching of the coming of Christ is not just some academic exercise, it is a truth that should stir us to action. It should bring a sense of purpose to our lives, and peace to our hearts.

- **It is a great incentive to holy living**, "All who have this hope in him purify themselves, just as he is pure." (1 Jhn 3:3, see also 2 Pet 3:11-12).
- **It encourages us to perseverance and watchfulness**, "so that when he appears we

may be confident and unashamed before him at his coming." (1 Jhn 2:28, see also Mat 24:44).

- **It gives a clear warning to unbelievers**, "This will happen when the Lord Jesus is revealed from heaven in blazing fire with his powerful angels. He will punish those who do not know God and do not obey the gospel of our Lord Jesus." (2 The 1:7-8).

- **It offers comfort to believers in time of bereavement**, "For the Lord himself will come down from heaven, with a loud command ... we who are ... left will be caught up together with them in the clouds to meet the Lord in the air. And so we will be with the Lord forever. Therefore encourage one another with these words." (1 The 4:16-18).

Assignment
What encouragement should believers receive from the truth of Christ's return?

Signs of Christ's coming

Even though the disciples did not know exactly when Christ would come again, he had instructed them to live in a way that showed they were ready for his coming. Jesus also gave them signs that would indicate the nearness of his return.

- **The gospel must be preached to all the nations**, "And this gospel of the kingdom will be preached in the whole world as a testimony to all nations, and then the end will come." (Mat 24:14).

- **There will be great trouble in the world**, "because those will be days of distress unequalled from the beginning, when God created the world, until now--and never to be equalled again." (Mar 13:19-20).

- **False prophets and Christs will lead some astray**, "For false messiahs and false prophets will appear and perform great signs" (Mat 24:23-24).

- **Disturbance in the heavens** (may be literal or speak of empires falling), "There will be signs in the sun, moon and stars. On the earth, nations will be in anguish" (Luk 21:25-27).

- **A man of lawlessness will be revealed**, "for that day will not come until the rebellion occurs and the man of lawlessness is revealed, the man doomed to destruction." (2 The 2:1,3-4).

- **Many Jewish people will be saved**, "Israel has experienced a hardening in part until the full number of the Gentiles has come in, and in this way all Israel will be saved. As it is written: 'The deliverer will come from Zion; he will turn godlessness away from Jacob'." (Rom 11:25-26). This should be actively looked for by the Church, because it will result in great blessing.

"The Word of God does indeed teach that there will be an intensification of evil at the end of the Age, for Satan remains the god of this Age. But we must strongly emphasise that God has not abandoned This Age to the Evil One. In fact the Kingdom of God has entered into This Evil Age; Satan has been defeated. The Kingdom of God, in Christ, has created the Church, and the Kingdom of God works in the world through the Church to accomplish the divine purposes of

extending his Kingdom in the world. We are caught up in a great struggle - the conflict of the Ages".

- Eldon Ladd 'The Gospel of the Kingdom' p.125

The glorious coming of Christ

The coming of Christ should be eagerly anticipated because it is to be a day of glory and blessing for those who love him, "while we wait for the blessed hope--the appearing of the glory of our great God and Saviour, Jesus Christ," (Tit 2:13). Yet it will be a day of terror and judgement on all those who have rejected the gospel (2 The 1:7-10).

On that glorious day Jesus will come with his holy angels. The bodies of those believers who have died will be resurrected, as glorious bodies, like that of Christ. The theme of the resurrection of believers was an important part of the faith of the early church. Paul gave detailed teaching on this vital matter to the church at Corinth, (1 Cor 15:35ff). Believers living on earth at that time will be changed and, together with all the resurrected believers, caught up to be with Christ (1 The 4:13-17). The fact that believers are said to be 'caught up' does not necessarily mean that they are taken away to heaven. It does mean that they will be linked with Christ in his reign over the earth.

One of the difficulties in understanding the events of the end time is that scripture sometimes seems to link the resurrection of believers and unbelievers together, "Do not be amazed at this, for a time is coming when all who are in their graves will hear his voice and come out-- those who have done what is good will rise to live, and those who have done what is evil will rise to be condemned." (Jhn 5:28-29, see also Dan 12:2). Other Scriptures appear to separate the resurrection of believers and unbelievers, "The rest of the dead did not come to life (until the thousand years were ended.) This is the first resurrection." (Rev 20:5).

The Millennial reign of Christ

There has been much disagreement among Christians over the nature of the millennial reign of Christ. However, there are Scriptures that speak of the authority of God and his Christ being demonstrated over this fallen world. In this period of a thousand years (whether exact or symbolic) believers will be linked with Christ in ruling the whole earth, and subduing it under his authority. The Bible does not give us exact details of this period, but it does give glimpses of a time of great blessing, under the reign of Messiah, "May he rule from sea to sea and from the River to the ends of the earth ... May all kings bow down to him and all nations serve him." (Psa 72:8-14). Isaiah saw a future age when, "Never again will there be in it an infant who lives but a few days, or an old man who does not live out his years; the one who dies at a hundred will be thought a mere child; the one who fails to reach a hundred will be considered accursed." (Isa 65:20). Isaiah also saw an idyllic picture (whether literal or figurative) of the animal kingdom, restored to a pre-fall state, "The wolf will live with the lamb, the leopard will lie down with the goat, the calf and the lion and the yearling together; and a little child will lead them. The cow will feed with the bear, their young will lie down together, and the lion will eat straw like the ox." (Isa 11:6-7, see also Zec 14:16-20).

Jesus promised believers, who overcame that they would rule over the nations, "To the one who is victorious and does my will to the end, I will give authority over the nations--" (Rev 2:26-27), see also the parable of Christ, (Luk 19:12-27). There is one passage in Revelation that speaks specifically of a thousand year period when Satan will be bound, and triumphant believers will reign with Christ, "He seized the dragon, that ancient serpent, who is the devil, or Satan, and bound him for a thousand years." (Rev 20:1-6). During that time, those that belong to Christ will be given great authority over the world, "Blessed and holy are those who share in the first resurrection. The second death has no power over them, but they will be priests of God and of Christ and will reign with him for a thousand years." (Rev 20:6).

Assignment

What is meant by 'The Millennial reign of Christ'?

The final judgement

God has already appointed His Son, Jesus, to be the judge of all people, "Moreover, the Father judges no one, but has entrusted all judgement to the Son," (Jhn 5:22), "For he has set a day when he will judge the world with justice by the man he has appointed. He has given proof of this to everyone by raising him from the dead." (Act 17:30-31, see also 2 Tim 4:1). The judgement day for unbelievers seems to come after the Millennial Reign of Christ, when they will be raised from the dead, "(The rest of the dead did not come to life until the thousand years were ended.) This is the first resurrection." (Rev 20:5).

The great day of judgement will be a terrible place for unbelievers, when the hearts and works of all will be exposed and judged, "Then I saw a great white throne and him who was seated on it. The earth and the heavens fled from his presence, and there was no place for them. And I saw the dead, great and small, standing before the throne," (Rev 20:11-13). For those who reject the gospel and rebel against God the end will be the lake of fire, "Anyone whose name was not found written in the book of life was thrown into the lake of fire" (Rev 20:15). The judgements of God will be righteous and will include degrees of punishment in accord with the deeds that have been done, "The dead were judged according to what they had done as recorded in the books." (Rev 20:12, cp. Luk 12:47-48). We are taught that there is a final judgement for all people. This assures us that evil cannot triumph and that all the wrongs of life will ultimately be dealt with.

Believers too will be judged according to their works, "For we will all stand before God's judgement seat." (Rom 14:10-12, see also 2 Cor 5:10). This judgement will not lead to final condemnation, because God does not remember our sins any more, "Very truly I tell you, whoever hears my word and believes him who sent me has eternal life and will not be judged but has crossed over from death to life." (Jhn 5:24). The assessment of believers will be linked with rewards, or the lack of them, which will differ in degree from one to another, "If what has been built survives, the builder will receive a reward. If it is burned up, the builder will suffer loss but yet will be saved--even though only as one escaping through the flames." (1 Cor 3:13-15). It will all be in keeping with the deeds we have done on the earth. However, in our final state there will be a fullness of joy in every believer.

Assignment

What happens to unbelievers at the final judgement?

The new heavens and earth

This world has seen suffering and injustice on a vast scale for thousands of years. Even with all that God has accomplished in his Son, and the revelation of his grace, evil still persists. God promises to do away with this present order of things, by creating a new heaven and earth which will be full of righteousness, "But in keeping with his promise we are looking forward to a new heaven and a new earth, where righteousness dwells." (2 Pet 3:13, see also Isa 66:22). Peter describes the 'putting away' of the old order of things in catastrophic terms, "But the day of the Lord will come like a thief. The heavens will disappear with a roar; the elements will be destroyed by fire, and the earth and everything done in it will be laid bare." (2 Pet 3:10). Believers will dwell on the renewed earth, in the Holy City, "Then I saw a new heaven and a new earth, for the first heaven and the first earth had passed away, and there was no longer any sea. I saw the Holy City, the new Jerusalem, coming down out of heaven from God, prepared as a bride beautifully dressed for her husband." (Rev 21:1-2).

The Scripture makes very clear that God has an ultimate future for believers, which will be very glorious. It is so spectacular that the apostle says it is not possible for us to imagine it all, "Eye has not seen, nor ear heard ... the things that God has prepared for those who love him" (1 Cor 2:9).

Our new resurrection bodies will be part of that renewed creation, when all the effects of sin and suffering will be done away with, "He will wipe every tear from their eyes. There will be no more death or mourning or crying or pain, for the old order of things has passed away" (Rev 21:1-5). It seems that a physical earth will reveal the paradise of God. There will be "the marriage supper of the Lamb" (Rev 19:9), and we will have access to the "tree of life" (Rev 22:2). In this remarkable place, God will work out his great purpose through his people, "There will be no more night. They will not need the light of a lamp or the light of the sun, for the Lord God will give them light. And they will reign for ever and ever." (Rev 22:5).

Notes

God's Eternal Purpose

Appendix 1

Problem Texts in the Bible

There are some texts in the Bible that seem to contradict each other. Because of this, some have tried to ridicule the Bible calling it an unreliable book which is full of mistakes. A closer look at most of the texts will show that there is no real contradiction. However, there are a few texts which are not so easily explained. As Christians we hold to the infallibility of the original manuscripts. We acknowledge that there may be some very small problems, in a few texts, due to copyist errors. However, those very small mistakes do not affect any of the teaching of the Bible and does not call doubt on the rest of the book. We list below seven examples which are typical of the problem texts.

1. It is alleged that Genesis 1 and Genesis 2 contain two different accounts of the creation of the world which cannot be reconciled.

    There is no contradiction between the two accounts. We have to see that they are not written in a Western style but a Hebrew style. The Hebrews often did not write chronologically but logically. Chapter one gives the full story of creation, and then in Chapter two the writer goes back and gives further details of part of it.

2. Genesis 4:17 mentions Cain's wife. The query is raised as to how Cain had a wife seeing that there were only three people living in the world.

    Genesis 5:3-4 tells us that Adam and Eve had many children. In the early ages of mankind it was acceptable to marry a close relative (later forbidden under the law) so Cain would have married his sister.

3. Most problem texts have to do with the record of numbers e.g. in Numbers 25:9 24,000 people are said to have died in a plague whereas, in 1 Corinthians 10:8 Paul says 23,000 died in the plague

    Look a little closer and you will see that Paul says 'There fell in one day 23,000' whereas the account in Numbers records the number for the whole plague

4. 2 Samuel 21:19 says that Elhanan the Bethlehemite killed Goliath the Gittite but we all know that David killed Goliath in 1 Samuel 17.

    The answer is provided in 1 Chronicles 20:5 which tells us that Elhanan killed Lahmi the brother of Goliath. The words 'brother of' are either missing in the text of Samuel, or Goliath is being used as a family name covering the brothers.

5. In 2 Samuel 24:1 The Lord is said to stir up David to take a census of Israel. However,

in 1 Chronicles 21:1 it says that Satan stirred up David to take the census.

There is no real problem or contradiction. The Bible makes it plain that God can use Satan to accomplish his will. The outcome is that God stirred up David, but he did it through Satan.

6. In 2 Samuel 24:13 David is given the choice of 7 years of famine, 3 months before the enemy or 3 days plague. In 1 Chronicles 21:12 David is said to have the choice of 3 years of famine etc.

In Hebrew numbers are written using letters of the alphabet. The Hebrew letter for three is almost the same as for seven, except for a tiny stroke. It is quite possible that a copyist error occurred in this text.

7. Mark 10:46 says that Jesus healed Bartimaeus on his way out of Jericho. In Luke 18:35 we are told that Jesus healed Bartimaeus as he approached Jericho.

Recent archaeological digs have shown that there were two small communities close to each other both called Jericho. Jesus was obviously leaving the one community and crossing to the other.

God's Eternal Purpose

Appendix 2
Bible Reference Abbreviations

Old Testament

Gen	Genesis	Hos	Hosea		
Exo	Exodus	Joe	Joel		
Lev	Leviticus	Amo	Amos		
Num	Numbers	Oba	Obadiah		
Deu	Deuteronomy	Jon	Jonah		
Jos	Joshua	Mic	Micah		
Jdg	Judges	Nah	Nahum		
Rut	Ruth	Hab	Habakkuk		
1 Sam	1 Samuel	Zep	Zephaniah		
2 Sam	2 Samuel	Hag	Haggai		
1 Kgs	1 Kings	Zec	Zechariah		
2 Kgs	2 Kings	Mal	Malachi		
1 Chr	1 Chronicles				
2 Chr	2 Chronicles				
Ezr	Ezra				
Neh	Nehemiah				
Est	Esther				
Job	Job				
Psa	Psalms				
Pro	Proverbs				
Ecc	Ecclesiastes				
SoS	Song of Solomon				
Isa	Isaiah				
Jer	Jeremiah				
Lam	Lamentations				
Eze	Ezekiel				
Dan	Daniel				

New Testament

Mat	Matthew
Mar	Mark
Luk	Luke
Jhn	John
Act	Acts
Rom	Romans
1 Cor	1 Corinthians
2 Cor	2 Corinthians
Gal	Galatians
Eph	Ephesians
Phi	Philippians
Col	Colossians
1 The	1 Thessalonians
2 The	2 Thessalonians
1 Tim	1 Timothy
2 Tim	2 Timothy
Tit	Titus
Phm	Philemon
Heb	Hebrews
Jam	James
1 Pet	1 Peter
2 Pet	2 Peter
1 Jhn	1 John
2 Jhn	2 John
3 Jhn	3 John
Jde	Jude
Rev	Revelation

Additional

cp = Compare the two passages referenced
ff = Also read the following verses for a fuller picture

Bibliography

Chadwick, Samuel, "The Way To Pentecost"
London: Hodder and Stoughton Ltd. reprint January 1934.

Tozer, A. W. "The Knowledge of the Holy"
England, Kent: STL Books, reprint 1981 ISBN 0 903843 45 5.

Lloyd-Jones, Dr. Martin "God The Father, God The Son" Great Doctrines Series Vol.1
London: Hodder and Stoughton 1996. ISBN 0 340 65165 2

Ladd, George Eldon, "The Gospel Of The Kingdom"
USA: William B. Eerdmans Publishing Company 1959. ISBN 978 0 8028 1280 3

Holland, Tom "Romans, The Divine Marriage"
USA: Pickwick Publications 2011. ISBN 13:978 1 60899 809 8

Hughes, Philip Edgcumbe, "The True Image"
England: Inter-Varsity Press 1989. ISBN 0 85110 680 3

Calvin, John, "Calvin's Institutes"
Grand Rapids, Mich: Associated Publishers and Authors Inc. A150-00067-4

Grudem, Wayne, "Bible Doctrine"
Inter-Varsity Press, Published by Zondervan 1999 ISBN 0-85111-594-2

Westminster Confession of Faith.
The English text is taken from the second edition which appeared under the title, 'The Humble Advice of the Assembly of Divines, now by Authority of Parliament sitting at Westminster, concerning a Confession of Faith: 1647. As used by e-sword.

The Westminster Shorter Catechism
Prepared by the Westminster Assembly in 1647. As used by e-sword

The Holy Bible, New International Version.
Copyright © 1973, 1978, 1984, 2011 by International Bible Society.
The "NIV" and "New International Version" trademarks are registered in the United States Patent and Trademark Office by International Bible Society.